Introducing Story-Strategic Methods

Introducing Story-Strategic Methods

Twelve Steps toward Effective Engagement

ROBERT STRAUSS

WIPF & STOCK · Eugene, Oregon

INTRODUCING STORY-STRATEGIC METHODS
Twelve Steps toward Effective Engagement

Wipf & Stock
An Imprint of Wipf and Stock Publishers
199 W. 8th Ave., Suite 3
Eugene, OR 97401

www.wipfandstock.com

PAPERBACK ISBN: 978–1-5326–1316-6
HARDCOVER ISBN: 978–1-5326–1318-0
EBOOK ISBN: 978–1-5326–1317-3

Manufactured in the U.S.A.   MARCH 1, 2017

Contents

Contents

List of Tables

List of Figures

Acknowledgments

FOR HER ENCOURAGEMENT AND loving support throughout a lifetime of work and service, during long hours of graduate studies at Biola University's School of Intercultural Studies, and over months of unending research and writing, I want to express my deepest love and gratitude to my wife Carole. Few know all that you have done to help make this publication happen.

An editor and writer without equal, I am so grateful for my son Christopher who spent many hours poring over drafts, pondering terms, concepts, and theoretical frameworks, and sharing invaluable suggestions for improvement. Talented and educated far beyond his father, I am indebted to him for his inimitable contributions to this work and others. Thank you for your kind manner throughout the process of editing and rewriting.

At Biola University's School of Intercultural Studies, Dean Doug Pennoyer was instrumental in my acceptance into the program of missiological research, and Professor Tom Steffen was crucial in providing needed guidance as my dissertation advisor. Many thanks to you both for believing in me.

Colleagues at Worldview Resource Group have been supportive and engaged throughout all aspects of developing this book series entitled "There is More to the Story". Thank you, Mike Matthews and John Cosby.

My business partner at Global Perspectives Consulting has trusted me with the company she founded and motivated me toward increased effectiveness in all areas of life and work. Now she has her turn as a PhD candidate in the Hugh Downs School of Human Communication at Arizona State University. Thank you, Elena Steiner.

Finally, I am forever grateful to the late Hugh Eaton, Co-Founder of The Weather Channel and mentor.

Introduction

ABOUT THIS BOOK SERIES

AN EPISODE IN THE Gospel of Mark Chapter 13 begins like this: "As Jesus was leaving the temple, one of his disciples said to him, 'Look, Teacher! What massive stones! What magnificent buildings!'" (NIV). Undoubtedly, to the disciples from Galilee, the Jerusalem Temple was magnificent. And indeed it was. The edifice of the Herodian Dynasty is now considered an architectural wonder of the ancient world.[1] The walls were sixteen feet thick and rose to some nine stories. Stones measured sixteen by forty feet and weighed over 500 tons.[2]

Jesus summarily replied to the disciple (Mark 13:2, NIV), "Do you see all these great buildings? Not one stone here will be left on another; every one will be thrown down." A staggering prediction! How? When? By whom? There was no possible way this could happen! There had to be more to the story.

Subsequently in the same chapter, Mark tells us that Jesus and some of his disciples departed the city and sat opposite the Temple on the slopes of the Mount of Olives. There, with the Temple in clear view to the west across the Kidron Valley, Jesus explained what he meant and what was to come. Indeed, there was more to the story!

"There is More to the Story" is a series of books, a compilation of resources provided by consultants from Worldview Resource Group, a service organization that equips mission leaders in a story-based worldview

1. Edersheim, *The Temple*, 38.
2. Barton, "Temple of Herod," Jewishencyclopedia.com.

approach to cross-cultural ministry. Along with their global experience as field practitioners, the authors in the series are equally grounded in academic research.

The content in the series challenges prevalent thinking and current methodologies employed in evangelism and discipleship around the world. The authors write that too often the Gospel story is presented before the evangelist is adequately aware of the hearers' stories. In fact, some even consider such awareness unnecessary. Added to this naivety is an ineffective presentation of a truncated biblical story.

Said succinctly, would-be evangelists do not say enough and do not amply know whom they address. Since saying it succinctly is not enough, we wrote this series, which attempts to preempt the rapidly-prepared, quick-fix approaches that tell only portions of the biblical story. In their place, we present a comprehensive, viable, and thoroughly biblical alternative.

ABOUT THIS BOOK IN THE SERIES

This book introduces cross-cultural workers to a proven methodology for effective ministry across cultures. The methodology is field-derived. It is grounded in observable data from various parts of the world. At the same time, it is also supported by precedent literature, not only in the discipline of missiology but also more broadly.

This is not simply another book about storytelling. There is more to our approach than story. This book embeds storytelling in a broader methodology of communication across cultures. Storytelling itself is not the whole approach. It is one component integrated into the whole.

It is our hope that the book is fresh, engaging, thought provoking, cutting-edge, and destined to make a difference in the world of missions.

ABOUT THE TERMINOLOGY IN THIS BOOK

Field practitioners will recognize most of the terminology in the book. Nevertheless, it is important that we operationally define several key terms. Here are some of the more important:

- Evangelism—While all of us know that *evangelism* involves spreading the Christian Gospel, especially to people who have not previously had an opportunity to hear and understand it, we endorse missiologist

David Hesselgrave's argument that evangelism is more than simply telling or announcing. His concern is "with *communicating* Christ across cultural barriers to the various peoples of the world" (emphasis added).[3] True evangelism requires communication. The "sender" tells and the "receiver" understands. If the receiver does not understand, is not "moved", neither communication nor evangelism has taken place. So, if evangelism requires communication, then irreplaceable components of communication are at play in evangelism. The book will explore the theory of communication in detail.

- Discipleship—Matthew 28:18–20 is clear that Jesus commands his followers to make disciples. *Discipleship* means the growth of the follower of Christ in his or her relationship with God. It involves discipline and devotion. The series and this book recognize that our mission is making disciples who glorify God with their lives, not tabulating numbers of those who profess to be converts.

- Church Planting—The emphasis of the New Testament pertains to planting local churches region by region. The details of the biblical account are quite clear. The tasks take time. They are costly. Relationships must be formed. There is both preaching and teaching. Followers of Christ are developed over time. Lives and communities are changed. There are joys and sorrows. Leaders emerge who meet qualifications. And much more. Note that the authors see *church planting* as an integral part of advancing the Kingdom of God. We do not support the notion that church planting is now passé.

- The Gospel—As per First Corinthians 15:1–4, the *Gospel* is the good news of Jesus Christ's death, burial, and resurrection for the redemption of lost humankind. It is not a compilation of theological propositions. It is a culmination of a salvation history story that begins in the beginning.

- Faith—*Faith* in the biblical sense is neither self-confidence nor self-efficacy. To the contrary, faith is an attitude of certainty in something outside of oneself. Correspondingly, actions accompany the attitude. Faith is not so much a feeling as it is a sureness of the validity and reliability of something outside of oneself. Of course, we are speaking of God and his Word. One may feel fear but not permit that feeling to

---

3. Hesselgrave, *Communicating Christ Cross-Culturally*, 26.

control one. In the midst of feeling fear one can take a step of faith and thereby please God.

- Story—*Story* includes an actual plot (storyline) with characters in a time and place. It is the events that really happen. It is an experience. Analysts today who delve into and dwell only in the analytical elements of story (setting, symbols, or the like) often fail to understand what story is. Its key is not a component part, but what story does as a whole, that is, a recreation of lived experiences. The aesthetic is more important than the analytic.

- Narrative—In contrast to story, *narrative* is merely someone's account of the event that really happens. An event may be true but the narrative told about it may or may not be.

- Language—*Language* is the symbols and sounds used to communicate. Language provides a productive system for meaning transfer. It is recursive, that is, it repeats itself assuring that meaning is consistent. And, remarkably, it provides a means to share about things that may not be immediately present temporally and spatially.

- Culture—The series defines *culture* as "the learned, shared patterns of perception and behavior".[4] Culture has a depth to it—outward observable behaviors, socio-cultural institutions, values, and core worldview assumptions. Without a background in cultural anthropology, some mistakenly equate culture and worldview as the same. They are not.

- Worldview—This term refers to the narrative-grid through which one sees and interprets all aspects of life.[5] Sometimes *worldview* seems too complicated to consider but it is always too important to ignore. Worldview lies beneath all the layers of culture noted above.

- Metanarrative (the grand narrative)—Research shows that narrative is the basis for all meaning.[6] Controlling narratives emerge over time to explain the past, justify the present, and give trajectory to the future. A collection of controlling narratives among a group of people ultimately evolves into a big picture explanation of life . . . a *metanarrative*. The third book in the series by Michael Matthews goes deeper into the role of metanarrative in mitigating worldview.

4. Strauss, "Culture," Gpccolorado.com.
5. Strauss, "Worldview," Gpccolorado.com.
6. Bradt, *Story as a Way of Knowing.*

Readers may find that some of the content in this book is academic. It is! That is because we have assumed our readers are well educated and open to new strategies for ministry.

ABOUT THE ASSUMPTIONS CONCERNING THE READER

In writing this book, and the entire series, the authors assume that readers have been educated at a basic seminary level (graduate level studies) and are currently involved in cross-cultural ministry. So, any one of the books in this series is not "that book" one buys at the airport for an amusing sleepy read during the flight. Much of the content of this book may require reflection. It will challenge underlying assumptions. At times with intention it will be analytical. You may even need to look up the meaning of a word or two in the dictionary, a throwback to an earlier time when people discovered new terminology and theories in what they were reading.

ABOUT THE ARRANGEMENT OF THIS BOOK

The content of this book is divided into two parts and ten sections. The book begins by briefly describing a ministry context of the global mission enterprise. Through innumerable means and by countless followers of Christ, the story of the Bible is being told to all people. In the recent history of Christian expansion, storytelling has dominated the delivery of the Good News. But it turns out that storytelling is not a panacea. The book exposes the needs in current approaches and introduces a solution for a path forward. The book ends with a uniquely extensive bibliography indebted to multiple disciplines of research.

CHAPTER 1: DESCRIBING THE CONTEXT

In the first book of the series "There is More to the Story", Tom Steffen details the current cross-cultural ministry context in which storytelling is employed. Chapter 1 of this book retells one single story from Morocco that is a narrative meme of the current context of global missions. Check out the story. It says it all.

CHAPTER 2: EXPOSING THE NEED

There is more to the story. Abruptly sharing story bits is rarely effective in intercultural communication. In what way is there more? The whole story needs to be told. Further, suddenly entering a host society as a stranger and assuming the right to speak is rarely, if ever, characterized by locals as love and respect. In what way is there more? The story context needs to be considered. Who are these people? What is their history? How have they suffered? Suffering perpetrated by whom? What do they value? What are their core assumptions about what is and is not reality? There are needs in current approaches to cross-cultural ministry. See what they are. Chapter 2 exposes the need.

CHAPTER 3: ANALYZING THE NEED

The needs and their resulting problems exposed in Chapter 2 have happened for a reason. They are the result of choices. The authors in the series argue that underlying assumptions are the culprits. Studying what evangelists do in the context of ministry and why they do it forms the basis for the analysis of these assumptions. This chapter analyzes the underlying theories of current storytelling approaches. The thesis of the chapter is that, as cross-cultural workers, we should clearly understand *why* we do what we do. And, any supporting empirical and statistical evidence of effectiveness must be valid and reliable. We should not say, "Well, the Holy Spirit will cover for me."

CHAPTER 4: INTRODUCING A SOLUTION

This chapter introduces a solution grounded in empirical research. It presents a twelve-step methodology and briefly describes each step. There is a chronology to the method. It takes time and unfolds over time. It has starting and ending points. There is a procedure to the method. The twelve steps are carried out systematically. No, these are not twelve steps in a recovery program. Review Chapter 4 to see what WRG proposes as a novel approach.

CHAPTER 5: MAKING THE CASE

While storytelling is no panacea, it is a key component in effective communication across cultures. Chapter 5 makes the case for storytelling while at the same time demonstrating how it is embedded in a holistic methodology of cross-cultural ministry. Students of storytelling will recognize well-known, important authors in this chapter. Additionally, you will see new writers, some who are speaking about the concepts of story and communication but from disciplines seemingly removed from missiology.

CHAPTER 6: EXAMINING A SOLUTION—STEPS 1-5

Chapter 6 unpacks the details of the first five steps in the twelve-step methodology. These steps include investigation, introductions, modeling the life of the Lord Jesus in front of people who may or may not know him, learning stories and how to tell them with locally familiar forms and function, and analyzing those stories to determine who people are, their values, structures, and function. Reflect on why WRG argues for these preliminary steps prior to introducing Jesus.

CHAPTER 7: EXAMINING A SOLUTION—STEPS 6-9

Building on the initial steps, this chapter continues with an understanding of a people's big picture story. It is in this context, having built authentic relationships and with acquired insights, that the cross-cultural storyteller is ready to speak. The contextualized biblical story is shared and lived. Step 9 stresses the importance of "telling to Teach" (*t*2T). It is not enough to simply tell or announce. That is neither evangelism nor discipleship. Check out the *t*2T approach.

CHAPTER 8: EXAMINING A SOLUTION—STEPS 10-12

Chapter 8 explains the three concluding steps. We must validate that communication has actually taken place. The book shows how to do that in a cross-cultural setting. One cannot assume that communication has taken place. In fact, it is best to assume it has not. To perpetuate the expansion of the Kingdom of God, locals are trained and discipled. It will be through these new disciples that the local storyland will be reached.

CHAPTER 9: ANALYZING A SOLUTION

Having meticulously laid out the twelve steps in the methodology, the author steps back to analyze the solution offered in the book. What are its underlying theology, philosophy, and strategy? To what degree do you agree with WRG's stated theology and strategy?

CHAPTER 10: ANTICIPATING THE FUTURE

As we look to the future, we must be aware of what we do and why. The chapter provides a series of reflective questions to help with that awareness. Answers should move the reader toward increased effectiveness. The book calls for five paradigm shifts in the future. While book one in the series explored paradigms that have already shifted, this book ends with a call for more.

ABOUT WHAT IS NEXT

There is more. As you continue to read, honestly consider what is described and exposed. Is the story we tell your story also? Truly ponder the analyses of both the need and solution. Carefully reflect on the validity of each step in the proposed solution. Our prayer is that this book will equip you toward greater effectiveness in your cross-cultural ministry and more joy as you live to glorify God.

PART ONE

Acknowledging Ambiguity

1

Describing the Context

THERE IS MORE TO THE STORY

In Reza Aslan's book, *There is no god, but God,* the story is told on pages *xviii-xxi* of a conductor confronting a young American couple on a train bound to the interior city of Marrakesh from Casa Blanca on the Atlantic coast. In the story the conductor is upset and speaking loudly in Arabic, impacted by his Berber dialect. An economic center in West Africa, Marrakesh is a city dating from the Berber Empire with a population of about one million people.

Living now in California, but from the country of Iran, Aslan tells the story from his own perspective as a visitor in Morocco for several months. He is awakened from a rumbling slumber by a burst of conversation that he describes as a clap of thunder. It is coming from the adjacent compartment, loud enough to be heard over the roar of the train. Aslan says it sounded like a Moroccan authority was reprimanding someone and asking for passports.

The story goes something like this, but here it is retold fictitiously from the point of view of the conductor. However, the essence of the story is true.

The conductor had seen the young couple enter the First-Class compartment of Car 2 just after 8 PM in the evening. Departure from the train station in Casa Voys was at 20:50 with a normal arrival into the city of Marrakesh at midnight, three hours later. The train would make four stops along the way. Most passengers slept on this last run of the day from Casa Blanca. He did not know for sure at first, but assumed they were Americans from their appearance. Both were tall with long hair. The woman wore a thin long skirt and tank top. Her shoulders were bared and hair uncovered. It was blond and disheveled. They had backpacks but the man also carried a medium size box.

As soon as they were settled into their seats, the man opened the box and retrieved several books. The conductor immediately recognized what they were—Christian Bibles. His fury was abrupt, not only at the proselytizing but also the nightclub style apparel. The foreigner handed a book to each compartment companion who graciously accepted it. The conductor knew what to do but waited until the train was fully boarded. Mostly businessmen filled Car 2. Another man caught the conductors eye. He appeared Persian but seemed to carry himself comfortably. Maybe he also spoke Arabic, the conductor wondered.

Shortly after departing from Casa Blanca, the conductor confronted the couple. The man and woman had nestled together in the corner of a seat near the window. Even though he could speak some French and a few words in English, the conductor spoke to the foreigner in Moroccan Arabic. He understood he must be forceful and uninterrupted.

Flushed, the foreigner responded in French at first, but quickly reverted to American English. The conductor knew it! They were Americans! He paid no attention to the foreigner's responses. He fervently urged him to stop distributing material offensive to Allah. As he admonished the man, the man responded in defensive anger. The conductor demanded to see their passports.

The conductor had not noticed his flank, but promptly the Persian businessman was at his side, speaking Arabic softly. The Persian begged the conductor to understand. The foreign man and woman were married, he said. They were Americans. The Persian said that the man was attempting to tell the conductor that they were simply sleeping and meant no mischief. The conductor indignantly countered, "This is not a nightclub!".

Again, the American nervously beseeched the businessman, "Will you please tell this man we were sleeping (*xix*)?" The young woman cried out in panic, and the American began taking out money to pay off the conductor so he would leave them be.

The Persian intervened once more and quietly shared with the conductor that he would stay with the American couple to make sure they did no further harm. With extreme reluctance, the conductor complied. In disgust, he departed and spat in English, "Christian!", his voice brimming with contempt.

He saw from a distance that the Persian businessman did move into the compartment. He spoke with the American couple. They seemed to be sharing some explanation with him. What he could not hear was that they told the Persian they were missionaries enroute to the country of Western Sahara through Marrakesh. The box they brought was filled with New Testaments translated into Arabic. They were distributing them as a means of sharing their faith with the people of Morocco as they traveled through the country. They did not speak Arabic and only a few words of French. They intended to share the Gospel in Western Sahara, also a Muslim nation where Arabic and Berber were spoken.

The conductor turned away in revulsion.

The young American couple was unaware, but there is more to the story. In the Prologue to *No god but God: The Origins, Evolution, and Future of Islam*, Reza Aslan (2011) describes the more complete story, including a bitter history of the region that not all understand, especially those coming in from the outside. Malcolm and Jennifer, the American couple on the train, had no lingering memory of the colonial endeavor, the "civilizing mission" that went hand-in-hand with the Christianizing efforts in the past.[1]

Most of the time locals do know and do remember the complete story, with fervency. Muslims resent the West and are suspicious of its people. In the Muslim world, many believe that there is a collision between the United States (and Israel) and Islam.[2]

So, one would not abruptly go into Morocco from the West. If one did enter the country, one would want to (re)build relationships, learn language, and (re)earn trust. Gifting the Christian New Testament in a local language would not be the first step.

THE SAME PLOT BUT DIFFERENT CHARACTERS AND SETTINGS

The story that Reza tells in his Prologue I have only heard once. It is in his book about Islam. But the plot we have heard countless times all over the world. In many ways Reza's plot crystalizes the context of modern Christian expansion. And, that context is the catalyst for this book.

---

1. Aslan, *No god but God*, xxiii.
2. Funk and Said, *Islam and the West*, 1–28.

A NEW STORY BUT . . .

Yes, the story of the Gospel of the Lord Jesus may be new in some locales, but to what degree do we realize that a rival story already exists in those locales, indeed in every locale? There is no place we go or group of people whom we approach where a story does not already exist. It is there and has been perhaps for centuries. The local and regional stories are deeply embedded in the lived experiences of local people. For the most part the local stories are trusted. They are retold again and again. From them people find meaning and direction for the future.

Furthermore, even if we are aware that a local story already exists, to what degree do we demonstrate respect for it and its role of making meaning and shaping a future in that locale? Respect across cultures requires time, relationships, trust, and the ability to effectively carry on human exchange with people who may think you, the outsider, are strange.[3] A key line from Reza's story may be from Malcolm when he said, "Will you please tell this man we were sleeping?" Malcolm may not have realized he was speaking metaphorically. The conductor already knew he was "asleep", asleep to history, to the local story, and to damaged relationships. He and his wife were also asleep to an effective approach to cross-cultural ministry.

This book entreats followers of Christ to awaken in the intercultural environment. It describes a way to effectively minister across cultures.

A NEW STORY AND . . .

There is more to the story. Abruptly sharing story bits is rarely effective in intercultural communication. In what way is there more? The whole story needs to be told. Further, suddenly entering a host society as a stranger and assuming the right to speak is rarely, if ever, characterized by locals as love and respect. In what way is there more? The whole story context needs to

3. The book *The Tender Soldier: A True Story of War and Sacrifice* written in 2014 by Vanessa Gezari tells the story of military anthropologist Paula Lloyd. Paula was assigned to a Human Terrain System (HTS) team near Kandahar, Afghanistan. In November 2008, a local man in the Maiwand Bazaar poured kerosene on Paula and set her on fire in an attempt to murder her. The story of HTS in Iraq and Afghanistan parallels Christian expansion. In those operational theaters soldiers were attempting to accomplish a mission among local people. The United States Army launched the HTS program (an unlikely marriage to anthropology) to help soldiers understand how to do their mission across cultures in a counterinsurgency environment. Over time it became clear that the degree to which culture was ignored was the degree by which missions failed.

be considered. Who are these people? What is their history? How have they suffered? Perpetrated by whom? What do they value? What are their core assumptions about what is and is not reality?

This book introduces cross-cultural workers to a proven methodology for effective ministry across cultures. It is not simply another book about storytelling. This book embeds storytelling in a much broader methodology of communication across cultures. Storytelling itself is not the system. It is but one component integrated into a whole approach.

ANTICIPATING WHAT IS TO FOLLOW

In Chapter 2 the author exposes the need in current approaches to cross-cultural ministry, especially approaches that assume storytelling is a standalone solution. In this series we argue that it is not a standalone solution. After exposing the need, Chapter 3 analyzes the need. Why is the need a need? Then, Chapter 4 introduces a solution and Chapter 5 makes a case for it. Chapters 6–8 describe the solution in detail. Chapter 9 analyzes the solution. Why this solution? In the end, Chapter 10 offers a way forward.

Keep reading to see what we say are the needs.

2

Exposing the Need

"Complex problems do not have simple solutions."

—A Chinese Proverb

COMPLEX SOLUTIONS ARE SOMETIMES necessary. Albert Einstein agreed, "A scientific theory should be as simple as possible, but no simpler".[1] Is storytelling by itself a solution too simple to address the complex problems of cross-cultural ministry? This book series says, "Yes". Are we arguing against storytelling? No, certainly not! We will argue for it, ardently. However, to suggest that almost any outsider can abruptly enter a host society, briefly tell a biblical story, and expectantly assume that insiders will abandon their historical "lived experiences"[2] and embrace this new story in repentance and faith is a solution that is too simple. It has typically not worked. This chapter presents evidence to that effect from four sources: (a) descriptions from Scripture, (b) empirical research from the field, (c) an analysis of culture, and (d) insights from historical literature. Figure 2.1 displays the four sources of evidence that expose the need.

---

1. This appears to be an adaptation of a statement Albert Einstein made on June 10, 1933 at the Herbert Spencer Lecture delivered at Oxford University.

2. Dilthey, *The Formation of the Historical World in the Human Sciences*, 24.

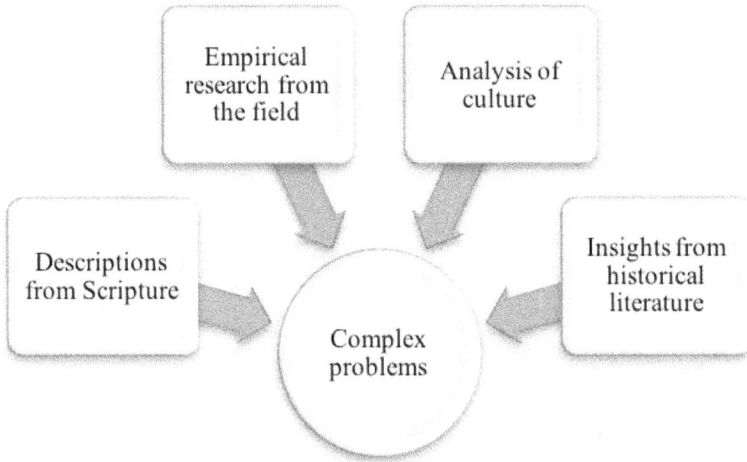

Figure 2.1: Exposing the Need

"There is more to the story" than simply storytelling. This book offers a solution that builds around the effectiveness of storytelling and incorporates a much more intricate framework of approaches to solve complex problems in concrete ways.

Part of any solution is defining the problem. This chapter attempts to do so. We begin with descriptions from Scripture about the difficulties that the cross-cultural worker encounters working with people.

DESCRIPTIONS FROM SCRIPTURE

While the Bible offers many cases of communication gone awry (or cases of the challenges of cross-cultural ministry), few passages capture the scope of the challenge as well as one in the Epistle to the Ephesians.[3] In his epistle to the church at Ephesus, the Apostle Paul describes the ministry tasks, objectives, expected responses from hearers of the Word, and the ministry difficulties faced by apostles, prophets, evangelists, and pastor/teachers. The difficulties are daunting. Consider to what degree every one of these difficulties is compounded across cultures and languages. The passage is Ephesians 4:11–25. Table 2.1 analyzes Ephesians 4:11–25. It identifies the ministry tasks. It clarifies the ministry objectives. It explains what is

---

3. *Plot* is not merely the sequence of events in the story (Kennedy et al., *Handbook of Literary Terms*, 115).

expected from the hearers. And, it describes the ministry difficulties. Note the progression in tasks, objectives, and responses. Note the constancy of the difficulties. The verse references from Ephesians 4 are provided as superscripts in the table.

Ministry Tasks	Ministry Objectives	Expected Responses from Hearers	Ministry Difficulties
Teach[21]	Community in Christ[12]	Hear[21]	Futile thinking[17]
Equip[12]	Christ as "head"[15]	Learn[20]	Dark understanding[18]
Build up[12]	Christlikeness goal[13]	Grow[15, 16]	Hardhearted[18]
	Unity attained[13, 25]	Put off old self[22]	Ignorance[18]
	Knowledge acquired[13]	Put away falsehood[25]	Callousness[19]
	Maturity[13]	Renew mind[23]	Immorality[19]
	Body functioning[16]	Speak truth[15, 25]	Greed[19]
	Body self-sustaining[16]	Love others[15, 16]	Impurity/corruption[19]
	Live as saints[12]	Put on new self[24]	Separated from God[18]
	God glorified[24]	Work together[16]	Immature[14]
		Do work of ministry[12]	Tossed[14]
			Susceptible[14]
			Deceived[14, 22]

Table 2.1: An Analysis of Ephesians 4:11–25

Ministry Tasks

The Epistle to the Ephesians tells a story. A human being, separated from God, deceived, immoral, and hardhearted, is to ultimately glorify God in a community of faith, living as a saint. Easy? Not in the least. This is complex at every level. There is more to the solution than simply, abruptly and briefly, sharing a biblical story. The Apostle Paul charges the leader to teach, equip, and build up. These are the ministry tasks. For what purposes?

Ministry Objectives

Cross-cultural ministry consultants are aware of the enormity of the objectives (see Column 2 in Table 2.1). They pertain both to the individual and a collective community of Christ followers, both of which are to mature. The objectives include spiritual qualities as well as ministry capabilities. They involve cognition, affect, acquired skills, self-actualization, and innumerable aspects of social relationships. Much is expected of the hearer.

Expected Responses from Hearers

Note the definitive and deliberate responses God expects from those who are recipients of the Good News (see Column 3 in Table 2.1). These verses in Ephesians 4 point to a final ministry goal far beyond evangelism. The ultimate objective is to make obedient disciples no matter how difficult the tasks or how long it takes (compare also Matthew 28:18–20 and 2 Timothy 2:2).

Ministry Difficulties

And, all of this activity is in the face of stated difficulties, none of which may be ignored and all of which are common to humankind anywhere in the world (see Column 4 in Table 2.1).[4] What is the ministry strategy and methodology for working with people who are hardhearted, ignorant, calloused, corrupt, and susceptible to deception? To repeat again, is the solution simply to tell several Bible stories over an abbreviated period of time? No. Such malfeasance would betray the divine calling of the apostle, prophet, evangelist, and pastor/teacher.[5]

4. Like *dramatic irony* some storytellers tell a new story into the host society but are completely unaware of the persistent power of the existing story already among the people group.

5. A Fashionable Model: It was the fall of 2003 on a Sunday morning in Lake Forest, California. My wife and I participated in a worship service at Saddleback Church where we were members. In the fall of each year, the church launched a new bold initiative for the coming year. That year a leader walked on to the stage with a Rubbermaid tub, which contained a tape recorder, cassette tapes of Saddleback sermons, and other artifacts from South Orange County "required" to do church planting across cultures. The Plan was that small groups of parishioners were to take the Rubbermaid tubs overseas during one- or two-week vacations to plant churches around the world. What had not been accomplished in the history of Christian expansion over the past two thousand years was going to be done by laypeople on holiday from Southern California. Where missiologists

Evidence from Scripture—and especially that in Ephesians—points to the complexity and difficulty of converting others, to the need for long, patient work, and rigorous, humane storytelling. In the next section, Scriptural evidence is buttressed by empirical evidence.

EMPIRICAL RESEARCH FROM THE FIELD

Empirical research for this chapter was gathered during the past decade through: (a) direct observation "in the field", (b) semi-structured interviews of church and mission leaders in West Africa, Indonesia, Thailand, Myanmar, India, Argentina, Chile, Paraguay, Guatemala, Honduras, Mexico, and

---

had failed, we, with our tubs, would succeed.

As if at a pep rally, the congregants grew feverish in their excitement that Orange County would in the coming months change the world. This did not seem odd to them. This is who they are. During the presentation there were standing ovations, fist pumps, and roars of excitement. While others stood, two people sat in their seats, shoulders drooped, heads down, expressions crestfallen, and hearts doleful.

I was asking myself, "To what lows had the advancement of the Kingdom of God fallen? Where would be the skilled proclamation of God's love? How well would parishioners know the Bible? Who would know the languages in the host culture? Who would be culturally adept? Not only proclamation, but in what ways would there be prolonged demonstration of the Gospel of the Lord Jesus Christ? What would be the process over time of making disciples and developing leaders to oversee regional communities of Christ-followers?" A dozen other questions swirled in my mind. Did Saddleback really think we would surmount the difficulties described by Paul in Ephesians 4 with this market driven offhanded approach? The answer is "yes". People either naively or dismissively assumed that brevity and the artifacts within the tub were the cure-all. The reality, however, is "no". Truncated methods do *not* work. How do we know? History and empirical evidence tell the true story.

A Past Model: The vision of Saddleback Church in Lake Forest, California, though unfledged, was not new. The English physician and founder of China Inland Mission (CIM), Hudson Taylor, spoke similarly in the 1860s. According to Taylor, China had at the time about fifty million families. If one thousand missionaries could reach fifty families per day, in three years the Gospel could be presented to all Chinese people.

German professor of mission at Halle University, Gustav Warneck writes that CIM sent out large numbers of evangelists in a short period of time trained with short courses. As many as were sent, returned. By 1900 almost all the inland stations were abandoned. Warneck concludes, "Worthy of respect as are the personal piety and self-sacrifice of these workers, yet, on the authority of reports deserving of credit, it must be doubted if all of them have been equal to their calling". Beyond the difficulties of the hearers described by Paul in Ephesians 4, we must consider also the difficulties of qualifying the storyteller in spiritual qualities and ministry capabilities. Then, out in the ministry setting, there are the difficulties of cross-cultural communication (Warneck, *Outline of a History of Protestant Missions*, 104).

Western Canada, and (c) feedback from focus groups. Everywhere, the results are the same. The stories are true. They have not been embellished. They are used with permission.

India

Bangalore (Bengaluru), Karnataka

Since 2004, Worldview Resource Group (WRG) has facilitated training modules in missiology in Bangalore, the capital of Karnataka. The India Institute of Missiology, directed for many years by the late Dr. C. Barnabas, sponsored most if not all of these learning events. Additionally, Worldview Resource Group taught academic courses at the South Asia Institute for Advanced Christian Studies. Hundreds of leaders from local churches, mission agencies, and missionary training centers have been students in the training modules at either MA or PhD levels.

Participants have come from all parts of India: Tamil Nadu, Kerala, Andhra Pradesh, Maharashtra, Gujarat, Odessa, and other locations. They represent all of India's major caste communities. One was a converted Roman Catholic priest. Another was formerly a high caste Brahman priest from Hinduism. Some had even traveled to Bangalore from Myanmar. All were followers of Christ. Each was involved in some leadership capacity out in the field related to church and missions.

The module topics included worldview, animism, folk religion, narrative, qualitative research methods, instructional design, and leadership across cultures. Generally, WRG facilitators begin with lecture, as is often expected in the local context, but as trust is built, facilitators convert the delivery style to storytelling accompanied by experiential learning activities.[6] All skilled facilitators understand the "cone of learning" where the degree of learning increases in proportion to the degree of learner involvement.[7]

Locals in India are skilled storytellers, especially in informal contexts. Because people in India are high-context communicators, stories always contain robust background with meticulous details that paint a picture of a concrete relational time/space context. Locals enjoy knowing who the

6. ELAs are debriefed using David A. Kolb's "Circle of Experiential Learning" with its four stages: concrete experience, reflective observation, abstract conceptualization, and active experimentation. Kolb's model moves from apprehension to comprehension, a process that is critical to a storytelling strategy. See also Strauss, "Experiential Learning."

7. See image of the "cone of learning" at http://www.tbointl.com/training.

hero is at the beginning of the story with plots of tension and resolution developed around that character after he (generally a male) is disclosed. Not infrequently, some story segments are silly, which brings comic relief to hearers who may live difficult lives.

These educated Christian leaders have been immersed in storytelling approaches, such as The Emmaus Road Message, from Good Seed International; Chronological Bible Teaching (now referred to as Foundational Teaching), from New Tribes Mission; or Bible Storying, from the International Mission Board. Libraries at missionary training centers in India contain printed volumes describing all of these approaches and more. Experts from abroad have facilitated training modules in the same. The India leaders are diligent in their study of Scripture. They love the Lord Jesus Christ and have committed their lives to Him amidst a culture dominated by Hindu philosophy and practice.[8]

It is from these local leaders in India that Worldview Resource Group has collected data. The India leaders themselves describe their own emic assumptions and personal behaviors. The data shared here is not from stories the leaders have told about subordinates or parishioners only. Their stories are also about themselves, rare glimpses into the lives of people who by nature conceal vulnerability amidst a culture of saving face.[9]

Here is what we have heard from these seasoned Christian leaders. If a rooster crows at an untimely moment during the day, one must return home, pray for protection, and then venture out again. The untimely crowing is a bad omen and bespeaks impending calamity, even unexpected death.[10]

It is advisable to sleep with one's face pointed to the east because the east is the source of good energy. Divine energy flows from the east. (Similarly, First Nations people in North America understand the sacredness of geographic directions. For them, east, the direction from which the sun rises and where light displaces darkness, is the source of positive energy.) If at all possible, a Hindu will position the puja room of worship in the east or

8. Regarding emerging leaders in the global mission enterprise, see Strauss, "The Emerging Geography of Global Christianity: New Places, Faces and Perceptions."

9. "She was like some ancient palimpsest on which layer upon layer of thought and reverie had been inscribed, and yet no succeeding layer had completely hidden or erased what had been written previously" (Nehru, *The Discovery of India*, 56).

10. Cultural anthropologists know this phenomenon is not unique to India. Stories are told of such beliefs throughout Europe during medieval times. It is also common in Chinese folklore.

northeast quadrant of the house. Again, this direction is the source of happiness, prosperity, health, wealth, and peace of mind. The idols in the puja room also face the same direction. As such, the design complies with Vastu guidelines in Hindu architecture (www.sanskrit.org). It is certain that the arrangement of the Old Testament wilderness tabernacle with its entrance to the east comports with Hindu thought and practice and supports the prevailing worldview assumption about divine energy originating in the east.

Connected in many ways to the India Institute of Missiology, a mission leader from the most prominent evangelical denomination in Myanmar tells the authors that in all the evangelism and discipleship endeavors in Myanmar not one outreach is addressing worldview. He considers this the most urgent need for local Christian workers. He cites history as far back as 200 years to the time of Adonirum Judson, a history he discloses as devoid of expertise in cross-cultural ministry.

Bidar, Karnataka

Dr. Jayakumar Ramachandran, Founder of Bible Believing Churches and Missions, trains young pastors in the north of the state of Karnataka and elsewhere. The authors have traveled with him to Bidar, a city tucked in the far corner of the state with Maharashtra to the west and Andhra Pradesh to the east. Locals in Bidar speak Kannada, the official language of Karnataka. But residents also speak Marathi, if they originate from Maharashtra, or Telugu, if they are from Andhra Pradesh. Because Bidar is such an important city in the history of Islam, many Muslims from the northwest have immigrated to the area, most of whom speak Urdu. The Gurdwara Nanak Jhira Sahib Sikh shrine is located in the city, a destination of as many as 30,000 pilgrims a day. Distinct tribal languages are spoken in the countryside surrounding the city. Muslims occasionally participate in Hindu and Sikh rituals as their worldview is mixed with an assortment of traditions and assumptions.[11]

11. "The missionaries had come to Umuofia. They had built their church there, won a handful of converts and were already sending evangelists to the surrounding towns and villages. That was a source of great sorrow to the leaders of the clan, but many of them believed that the strange faith and the white man's god would not last. None of his converts was a man whose word was heeded in the assembly of the people. None of them was a man of title. They were mostly the kind of people that were called *efulefu*, worthless, empty men. The imagery of *efulefu* in the language of the clan was a man who

Jayakumar's research in 2014 has shown that 80 percent of the evangelical church plants in this region and throughout India fail. He has pinpointed the reason. He demonstrates that church planters focus on evangelism, telling the story of Jesus, but devote little to no ministry activity to discipleship. He writes, "In general, 'discipleship' is an alienated agenda in the church-growth activities in India".[12] Initial followers of Christ who are excited to hear about Jesus eventually abandon the Christian faith in discouragement and turn back to an old order of things.

The authors have facilitated training modules among local pastors and cross-cultural workers based out of Bidar. Modules have focused on storytelling and the role of worldview in cross-cultural ministry. As elsewhere, locals are master storytellers as displayed over and again at lunch and tea breaks. We have shared stories, jokes across cultures (which do not always work well), laughed, and bonded through these informal times of enjoyable fellowship as followers of Christ. However, students have confided in the training facilitators that they have never been exposed to any instruction related to worldview and consequently have incorporated absolutely nothing related to worldview in their ministry approaches.

All the while, syncretism is rampant, and, as trainers define the term syncretism, local pastors offer story after story describing and proving its ubiquity, not only in the lives of those to whom they minister but in their own lives as well.

Before the worldview training, these pastors said they used pastoral authority in an attempt to squelch widespread syncretistic behaviors. They assumed that by authoritative force the pastor would be able to deter the behaviors. And they unknowingly assumed that by authoritative force the pastor would be able to displace the core worldview precepts of animism from the mind and heart of a person. To no avail! Local pastors and cross-cultural workers have confessed that their ministries are not effective beyond initial presentations of the Gospel. Parishioners are not growing in the faith. Few animistic practices have ended and, more seriously, the framework of thoughts underlying those practices remains entrenched.

Note carefully that local pastors did not explicitly know their own cultures. Previously, they were not equipped to address deeply embraced

---

sold his machete and wore the sheath to battle. Chielo, the priestess of Agbala, called the converts the excrement of the clan, and the new faith was a mad dog that had come to eat it up" (Achebe, *Things Fall Apart*, 143).

12. Ramachandran, *Current Political and Missions Landscape*, 284.

value dimensions and tacitly presumed core worldview assumptions. Their assumed biblical authority as a pastor was not locally derived. The authority was conferred on them by a "religion" from the "outside". As such, local culture embedded over time trumped their assumed authority. Neither their forcefulness nor faith displaced or deterred local folklore about personal spirit beings and impersonal spiritual forces.[13]

Dimapur, Nagaland

Locals say if a person is unexpectedly frightened, his human spirit will straightway depart from the physical body and settle in the countryside nearby. This occurrence is not uncommon among locals and is experienced too by followers of Christ. It is widely understood that the person must immediately go home and lie down to avoid illness. Thereafter, he will phone his pastor to report what has transpired. The pastor knows where to go and what to do. He will go into the countryside and perform an animistic incantation to retrieve the disembodied spirit. From the countryside he will transport the spirit, on his own back, to the home of the afflicted person where the human spirit will reenter the body, thus averting malady and infirmity.

Sixteen main languages are found throughout Nagaland's eleven districts. Over 90 percent of Nagas profess to be followers of Christ, evangelized a hundred years ago by Baptist missionaries who braved personal danger, disease, and inhospitable climates to share the Gospel of Christ with locals who previously had never heard of the Bible. The motto of the Nagaland Rebels is "Nagaland for Christ". Though almost all profess to be followers of Christ, many also retain core assumptions from traditional animism. Christianity serves more as a folk religion, that is, a veneer over the top of animistic values and worldview assumptions.

13. "All the men of the Ibo clan from the villages of Umuofia had been summoned by the elders to the marketplace to talk about the impact of the white Anglican missionary. Okika addressed the assembly: 'You all know why we are here, when we ought to be building our barns or mending our huts, when we should be putting our compounds in order. My father used to say to me, 'Whenever you see a toad jumping in broad daylight, then know that something is after its life.' When I saw you all pouring into this meeting from all the quarters of our clan so early this morning, I knew that something was after our life.' He paused for a brief moment and then began again. 'All our gods are weeping. Idemili is weeping. Ogwugwu is weeping. Agabala is weeping, and all the others. Our dead fathers are weeping because of the shameful sacrilege they are suffering and the abomination we have all seen with our eyes.' He stopped again to steady his trembling voice" (Achebe, *Things Fall Apart*, 203).

Locals have heard the piercing scream of diminutive human creatures, although no one says he has really seen one. These creatures live in forested areas beyond the villages inhabited by humans. They are approximately a half-meter tall with dreadlocks. They carry locally familiar weapons, diminutive also, by which they inflict harm on land, crops, animals, and humans. In fact, they *are* the cause of calamity and must be appeased by observance of taboos or some form of offering if taboos are violated. Pastors studying in the Masters of Divinity program at the South Asia Institute for Advanced Christian Studies have told me they themselves have heard the shrieks and know these beings exist out in the hilly woodlands. To venture into such areas at night is terrifying. The local people do not do it and neither do followers of Christ.

Indonesia

Yogyakarta, the Island of Java

When there is a death in the family, the human spirit of the deceased is displaced from the physical body but remains within the home of the extended family. After one week the spirit is transferred to an open area outside of town through an incantation ritual. After 1,000 days the human spirit is relocated to its final abode, again through ritual. That abode may be a sacred realm in a nearby mountainous region. Who officiates at these *selamatan* rituals? In the old order of things, the officiating of the rituals would be a function of the shaman. Do followers of Christ continue these ceremonies to help the human spirit migrate to its final abode? Yes. Who officiates? The pastor of the local church.[14]

Stories are told about men who turn into tigers and tigers into men. Stories told and believed by whom? By evangelical seminary leaders at the highest levels of authority.

---

14. Clifford Geertz provides the seminal analysis of selamatan death ceremonies on the Island of Java in a descriptive monograph published by the University of Chicago with research done under the auspices of Massachusetts Institute of Technology funded by the Ford Foundation (Geertz, *The Religion of Java*, 68). Also, see *The Potent Dead: Ancestors, Saints and Heroes in Contemporary Indonesia*, edited by Henri Chambert-Loir and Anthony Reid in 2002.

Latin America

One of the more common stories told throughout Latin America and among many Latinos who now live elsewhere is about the practice of *pasando el huevo* ("passing the egg"). A friend living in Germany who is from Northern Mexico learned the practice from her grandmother and mother. She has three children. When they are sick she prays to God and "passes the egg" over their bodies. She is a devout follower of God, is studying for a Master's degree in education, and is married to a high level administrator in the Department of Defense of the United States of America. Latina students at Regis University in Denver, Colorado, disclose that they practice *pasando el huevo*. Worldview Resource Group consultants who facilitate missionary training modules and provide consultation to mission leaders throughout Ibero-America hear of Christ followers and participants in the training modules who continue to "pass the egg" whilst deeply embracing its accompanying worldview assumptions.

What is *pasando el huevo*? Often it is related to the evil eye. If through the effect of the evil eye, a child becomes ill, the mother will retrieve a fresh raw chicken egg from food storage and pass it over the body of the child. In Latin America, healing/blessing prayers to saints or God (*benedicaria* in Italy and *suplicas* in Mexico) generally complement the curative practice of *pasando el huevo*. It is assumed that the egg, itself a living cell, has power to absorb maladies or negative energies from the human body—and does. A missionary nurse in Mexico recently reaffirmed her belief in the same.

After the first step in the ritual of passing the egg, the mother will crack open the eggshell and drop the yolk and egg white (albumen) into a glass of water, preferably warm. As the yellow yolk, albumen, and chalaza descend through the water to the bottom of the glass, the mother "reads" the descent (ease of breaking the eggshell, descent speed, lateral movement, component shapes, and final configuration at the bottom) and divines the problem within the child. All this she learns from her maternal relatives.

Many variations exist in the practice, such as washing the whole egg first with holy water, flushing the egg down the toilet after the ritual, or putting the egg under one's bed at night to absorb negativity.

The phenomenon of "the evil eye" (*el mal de ojo*) is as common in Latin America as it is throughout the Middle East. It is deeply embedded in cultures. Followers of Christ naturally and instinctively assume its truth. In antiquity Plato spoke of it (Phaedo 95b). The prophet stated that the influence of the evil eye is a fact (Sahih Muslim Book 26, Hadith Number 5427).

19

Another Hadith says that one third of the people in the grave are there due to the evil eye. It seems evident to those in such regions that the Bible also affirms the presence and power of "the evil eye":

Mark 7:23 "All these evils come from inside . . . " (NIV)

Proverbs 10:10 "Whoever winks maliciously causes grief . . . " (NIV)

Proverbs 20:8 "A King . . . winnows all evil with his eyes" (ESV)

Proverbs 28:22 "A man with an evil eye . . . " (NKJV)

What are symptoms of a curse from the evil eye? A baby suddenly starts crying, someone gets a headache, a business venture fails, the roof leaks, a car breaks down, there is an infestation of insects, someone gets sick, another person feels dizzy, or there is an untimely tragic death.

Ancient Romans would use rude sexual hand gestures to ward off the evil eye.[15] Parents today will defuse praise of a newborn to protect it. Others recite verses from the Bible or Qur'an. It has been said in Central America that a pastor's ability to protect parishioners from the evil eye and cure resulting maladies is in fact a spiritual gift. In Mexico one would be expected to touch a baby to void the effect of the evil eye. One may say, "Para no darle el mal de ojo".

Mexico

A Mexican missionary to the Tarahumara people recently shared with the authors a story about a boy that turned into a dog. Another missionary, training to serve as a church planter in Africa, told the story of a witch who lived nearby with the ability to shape shift. One evening when he was returning to his home, he became aware of a shadow following him. He knew it was the witch who had changed her form into an animal. Another local medical missionary in North Mexico told the authors that he would not venture out into surrounding local villages because the evil spirits there would surely harm him. Many indigenous pastors have told Worldview Resource Group trainers that Jesus Christ their Savior is a traditional spirit being just like others in their folklore.

A believer from Chihuahua who attended a local Christian fellowship began wearing a safety pin in her blouse. She was also notably pregnant. The reason for the safety pin is well known. Unless there is some type of

15. Corbeill, *Nature Embodied*, 61–62.

ornament used as a protective amulet against the power of a full moon, the baby will be subject to being born with a physical deformity.

Guatemala

A local church leader and missiological student in Guatemala shares that his life as a Christian is full of fear due to the stories told by his father and grandfather. One of the stories he told Worldview Resource Group was about a young boy who gathered eggs every day for his family. One day while gathering eggs at their small farm he accidently picked up a snake egg. Later this egg was cooked and the boy was the one who ate the snake egg. Shortly afterwards he began convulsing, foaming at the mouth, and gradually turned into a snake.

Peru

A lady in a Worldview Resource Group animism course in Cusco, Peru stated, "Now I see that for years, even as a Christian, I have harbored erroneous ideas about spirit powers that have affected my feelings and behavior. And I didn't even realize it."

Western Canada

Worldview Resource Group began facilitating training modules in Canada in the fall of 2007. These training events were hosted by InterAct Ministries of Canada and Northern Evangelical Mission of Canada and involved training in worldview-based, cross-cultural church planting methodologies. The training seminars continued for five years, with workers attending from the two hosting mission agencies plus others from North American Indigenous Ministries and SEND North. Combined, these mission organizations work in every section of Canada—from the Atlantic to the Pacific as well as from the US/Canada border to the Arctic Ocean. Of the trainees attending, approximately ninety percent were expatriate missionaries (from the United States and Canada) while ten percent were from indigenous First Nations tribes (primarily the Cree and Dene).

The training included instruction and discussion concerning worldview, animism, folk religion, narrative, chronological bible teaching, church planting, and culture acquisition. It generally followed the educational principles of andragogy and thus, in addition to the presentation of information, included significant times and techniques of garnering from the knowledge and experience of seminar attendees.

In speaking with those attending these training events it became clear that storytelling has a major place in the communication of both expatriates and indigenous people of Canada. It was the major means of communication at most after-dinner conversations. It was the communication mode of many personal examples and illustrations presented during the seminar discussions. And it had a major place in the sermons and devotionals our personnel attended—in these contexts the stories were added to a topical study or sermon to enhance or illustrate a point. The stories were overwhelmingly concrete, often dealt with everyday activities of life such as hunting and fishing, and habitually included a significant element of humor.

In the context of Bible storying, it is noteworthy to observe that many attending the WRG seminars during this five-year period had heard of and experimented with Chronological Bible Teaching. This methodology had been introduced into the Canadian mission scene in the early to mid-1980s, when some saw it as (perhaps) the panacea for teaching/training Canada's traditionally animistic First Nations people. For the most part, those that attempted this methodology followed the general outline presented in the Firm Foundations curriculum of New Tribes Mission.

This method of teaching was applied with little or no in depth intentional study of the tacit worldview assumptions of the target community or culture. Rather, only the methodology of chronologically presenting Bible stories was applied in place of a more topical approach that consisted of didactic teaching sprinkled with everyday story illustrations. Fast-forward twenty years from the mid-eighties. Most of those who had tried the Chronological Bible Storying approach found it helpful, but noted that it did *not* reap the results in Canada for which they had hoped and prayed. There was minimal worldview change among the target audience. For many of these sincere, biblically grounded, God-fearing, and Christ-following cross-cultural workers, this methodology became "one of those things we tried."

The following excerpts are a small sampling of personal stories heard from these expatriate and indigenous workers depicting core worldview assumptions:

1. "Whenever I drive by a cemetery, fear and dread come over me." This was shared with solemn emotion by an indigenous pastor of a local church in Western Canada.

2. "One day my wife and I were sitting in the living room when a bird flew into the window and died. We immediately became afraid and did not know what to do. My wife called her grandmother who told us what ceremony we needed to perform in order to keep someone in our family from dying as a result of this incident." Of course, this couple viewed the out-of-the-ordinary bird incident as a subtext—a death omen.

3. "It was only after a whole year that I could go to my father's house where my son had committed suicide. I could not go before that because of the fear I had of going to that house." In all of Canada the suicide rate among First Nations populations is twice the national average. Most suicides are severely intoxicated.

4. If someone has something in one's house that has been used in an animistic ceremony, that article has power in it and must be destroyed or removed in order for harmony and health to return to that house. There is a fairly widespread assumption that such cursed objects, perhaps even demon influenced, are the source of insomnia, nightmares, marital problems, infertility, migraines, and innumerable other maladies.

5. If I leave a Bible open in my room or if I sleep with a Bible under my pillow things go better for me. This assumption among First Nations people, regional Christian workers, and others is common all over the world. Followers of Christ in Latin America as well as Southeast Asia share the same belief.

6. "On the days that I forget or get too busy to have my devotions with the Lord things often do not go well." Rather than hearing the biblical story as a progressive revelation, followers of Christ learn about the blessings and curses associated with the Mosaic Covenant and assume its applicability to them. Therefore, in this scheme righteous acts, such as the practice of Christian disciplines, result in God's favor, not simply His emotional satisfaction with His children, but tangible earthly reward related to effectiveness, improved relationships, and perhaps even acquiring wealth. Failure to perform righteous acts incites God's disfavor and correspondingly punishment in the here and now.

7. "During the funeral proceedings, Christian leaders of the community had the coffin with the body in it brought into the community

hall through the window instead of through the door because of the spirit activity known to hover around doorways." It is common among many animists to assume that paranormal activity, particularly by malevolent spirits, congregated in low places along a pathway, vortexes, portals, or doorways.

8. "If I do not pray for food before I eat it, I will likely get sick." The Orthodox and Catholic Churches provide prescribed prayers, not restricted to meals, but also before bedtime, when waking, and before major events. For example, here is the prayer before meals, "Bless us, O Lord, and these your gifts which we are about to receive from your goodness. Through Christ our Lord. Amen."[16] In Islam, a follower of Allah is expected to pray individually and silently before and after a meal. It is evident this performance-based Christian lifestyle has been transferred to First Nations people through Christian missionaries.

While there are positive cases in Western Canada, and other parts of the world, what should be done to minimize communication noise to avoid these documented scenarios?

ANALYSIS OF CULTURE

The passage in Ephesians 4 describes the difficulties faced by a leader called by God to minister to human beings who are separated from God. The stories from the field confirm the ministry difficulties. Indeed, there is a darkened understanding. In this brief section, we look at the complex problems presented by culture itself. Note the challenges of simple communication across cultures.

Culture is the learned shared patterns of perception and behavior. Table 2.2 shows the ways underlying cultural values impact how a story is told and heard. The intended meaning of what is told may not match the derived meaning of what is heard. There are cultural values unique to the American and Northern Europe context, and the various subcultures within them. In fact, we may not even be aware of these values and how they impact what we tell and how we tell it.

In the same way, there are cultural values unique to the Majority World. People in the host societies likewise may not even be aware of their values and how they impact what they hear and tell. It is these differences that cause miscommunication.

16. From *Book of Blessings*, 1988, International Committee on English in the Liturgy.

America and Northern Europe			The Majority World	
Cultural values	Storytelling approaches	Miscommunication	Cultural values	Story hearing expectations
Individualism (originating from nineteenth-century utilitarianism in Europe)	I can tell a story without becoming part of a group	*Is the story foreign because it does not originate from nor align with local history?*	Collectivism	We must establish relationships before we have a right to share a story
Low-context communication	Story bits	*Is understanding fragmented minus a solid foundation?*	High-context communication	Whole story
Dichotomistic	Themes related to salvation are separated from Kingdom life	*Is understanding limited without clear solutions for the present life?*	Holistic	All themes within the story context relate to all of life
Time as commodity	Accomplish the goal hastily because time is valuable (as Benjamin Franklin said describing the spirit of capitalism, "Time is money.")	*Is the credibility of the storyteller and story diminished without a historical and relational presence?*	Time as opportunity	Build relationships as a basis for credibility
Future orientation	Be brief	*Does the biblical story fail to meet the standards of a "master narrative", therefore offers no real trajectory for the future?*	Past orientation	Go slowly

America and Northern Europe		Miscommunication	The Majority World	
Cultural values	Storytelling approaches		Cultural values	Story hearing expectations
Change	Small regard for past conventions	*Are the hearers not part of the new story without emotional connection to it?*	Tradition	Big regard for past conventions
Task	The story content is most important	*Is the integrity of the storyteller and story called into question?*	People	Relationships with people who hear the story are the foundation for everything
Exposure of vulnerability	No time needed to build trust	*Is the story credible, true, and honorable?*	Concealment of vulnerability	Much time needed to build trust
Status achieved through effort	I have the right to speak	*Is the storyteller shallow, hollow, and impertinent?*	Status ascribed thru birthright	I must earn the right to speak
Doing	Emphasis on behavior	*Do hearers easily adopt syncretistic behaviors but not really change who they are?*	Being	Emphasis on belonging
Directness	Urgency	*Is understanding incomplete?*	Indirectness	Delay
Topic and process	Share facts to be believed	*Does the biblical story become a folk religion but core identity markers remain unchanged?*	Relationship and identity	Build friendships and honor status
Low power distance	Anyone can tell a story at anytime	*Do the storyteller and story lack authority?*	High power distance	Only selected people have authority to share

America and Northern Europe

The Majority World

Cultural values	Storytelling approaches	Miscommunication	Cultural values	Story hearing expectations
Egalitarian	Everyone is part of all stories in some way	*Though interesting, is the biblical story about somewhere else and therefore does not apply in the particular setting of the locals?*	Hierarchical	Hearers do not assume they are part of the biblical story
Guilt/righteousness pattern	Legal emphasis	*Do hearers do something outwardly but are not transformed inwardly?*	Shame/honor pattern	Relational emphasis
Uncertainty avoidance	Reveal mystery as soon as possible	*Are hearers not drawn into the story?*	Comfort with ambiguity	Reveal over time in aura of mystery
Universalism	My story applies everywhere	*Is the story foreign?*	Particularism	My story only applies in my geographic area

Table 2.2: Miscommunication Due to Differences in Cultural Values

The missteps in communication highlighted in the center column of Table 2.2 occur everywhere all the time in cross-cultural communication. They are real and problematic, given the importance of the ministry tasks and objectives. Brevity and abruptness are no remedies. The storyteller who enters a host society but operates on cultural "auto pilot" simply repeats the patterns of culture from his homeland. He is not even aware he does so. He miscommunicates. Is he aware that he does so? The differences in culture are as definite and dramatic as any difference in language.

INSIGHTS FROM HISTORICAL LITERATURE

In what ways would insights from venerable researchers inform current missiological methodologies? Many researchers could be consulted. Below are two. For example, how familiar should a cross-cultural worker be with the research of Max Weber, the German sociologist? How does his thesis in *The Protestant Ethic and the Spirit of Capitalism* apply to cross-cultural ministry? What is the role of Weber's notion of *verstehen* in shaping the existing story in a host society? What impact does local history have in shaping personal and collective conscience? Answers to these questions are critical to mission methods.

Consider another forefather in the field of sociology, Emile Durkheim, the French researcher. Should contemporary storytellers incorporate Durkheim's four characteristics of society into the design and delivery of the biblical story? We feel they should. Here is a deeper look.

Durkheim sees four characteristics or dimensions of society that bespeak the continuity of the "conscience collective". He called them *volume*, *intensity*, *rigidity*, and *content*. Each impacts how easily, quickly, and completely a story hearer would embrace the new story of a storyteller, thereby abandoning the existing historical "conscience collective". Table 2.3 analyzes Durkheim's matrix and applies it to storying the Bible. Durkheim's four factors assume that the "conscience collective" is the totality of assumptions and values common to a group of people. These preexist and survive any one individual. They shape behavior.

Durkheim's factors	Description from his selected writings	Contempo-rary terms	Application to storying
Volume	The number of individuals within a society that tacitly or explicitly embraces core assumptions and common values.	Prevalent Dominant	Storytellers from individualistic societies do not accurately access the power of *volume*. Communal rituals reinforce a shared ontology and cosmology that are not easily dismantled.
Intensity	The degree to which people feel deeply about the core assumptions and common values. This factor speaks to the influence of the "conscience collective".	Passionate Devout	A story from the "outside" may only have minimal *intensity*. Georg Simmel, the German sociologist, would call the story "strange".
Rigidity	The clarity of definitions, especially prescribed social practices.	Precise Defined	Durkheim's research shows that if definitions are not clear, then *volume* and *intensity* will be lower.
Content	The form the "conscience collective" takes. For example, is it formatted as a religion?	Prescriptive Dogmatic	Durkheim's argument is that no other factor is as important as *content*, that is, the format. If a message from the outside does not have historical significance among the collective, it is largely pointless.

Table 2.3: Analysis of Durkheim's Four Factors

Durkheim adds, "There can be no society which does not feel the need of upholding and reaffirming at regular intervals the collective sentiments and the collective ideas which makes its unity and its personality. Now this moral remaking cannot be achieved except by the means of reunions, assemblies and meetings where the individuals, being closely united to one another, reaffirm in common their common sentiments".[17] Durkheim ties together the concepts of belief and ritual, both "social facts" he sees as institutions. Ritual helps to validate the cosmological order or worldview in the minds of participants.

If what Durkheim says is true, what is the biblical storyteller to learn from this writer of the nineteenth-century? What strategy then should be

17. Durkheim, *Selected Writings*, 474–75.

employed in order to share a new story, from the outside, that rivals the "conscience collective" with all its reinforcing activities and events that take place in the "lived experience"[18]? How will the cross-cultural worker manage *volume, intensity, rigidity,* and *content*? What experiential learning activities will be designed to move the story content toward belief, ritual, and ultimately a new cosmology? Again, these are real and challenging needs in cross-cultural communication.

CONCLUDING REFLECTIONS

In Ephesians 4, the Apostle Paul describes the difficulties of successful ministry. Cross-cultural storytellers around the world face them. In this chapter the needs have been exposed by empirical research from the field. Only a few real world examples were provided. Cross-cultural workers, intentionally or not, have neglected time, relationships, proficiency in language, investigation of culture, local history, shared values, and core worldview assumptions. By means of the "bits and pieces" approach to sharing the Bible, they have unwittingly manufactured syncretism. The empirical data show syncretism is widespread—and spreading wider.

The complex problems have been delineated through adept cultural analysis. The cross-cultural chasm is real. This is no fairy tale in which sprite or pixie dust closes the cultural gap. Venerable researchers in the past have exposed the complexity of the needs. Complex problems do not have simple solutions.

So what do we do? The next chapters analyze the need and offer a solution.

18. Dilthey, *The Formation of the Historical World in the Human Sciences*, 28.

3

Analyzing the Need

INTRODUCTORY REMARKS

THE PRECEDING CHAPTER DESCRIBES what the need is in the cross-cultural ministry context. The passage in Ephesians 4 indicates that the objectives and difficulties of ministry are multifaceted. Empirical research out in the field shows syncretism is rampant. This is a real and prevalent problem. Retention of paganism in any culture stifles spiritual growth individually and corporately. The complexities of ministry are compounded by culture. Cross-cultural communication is demanding. And too often cross-cultural workers in ministry may miss the benefit from the insights of social scientists across academic disciplines.

In this chapter we look at the *why* behind the *what*. Accordingly, we will identify and analyze some of the underlying philosophical and theological assumptions related to current storytelling strategies and methods. We are indebted to Ted Ward, Professor Emeritus of Educational Ministries and Mission at Trinity Evangelical Divinity School. Ward emphasizes "drivers" in cross-cultural ministry, arguing that one's methodology is always driven or shaped by one's strategic, philosophic, and, at root, theological assumptions (IFMA/EFMA Conference, 1992, Orlando, Florida).

Cross-cultural workers do not simply do things. Stated and unstated assumptions underlie methods, and even shape them. These assumptions are strategic, philosophical, and ultimately theological. Perhaps people do not stop and analyze the philosophical and theological underpinnings of why they do what they do. It requires mindfulness. Mindfulness has always been part of Buddhism. Today it has become more mainstream. Mindfulness psychology is part of leadership development in the business sector.

Preferring clarity to agreement, this chapter analyzes the underlying assumptions of current storytelling approaches. The thesis of the chapter is that the cross-cultural worker should clearly understand *why* he does what he does. And any supporting empirical and statistical evidence of effectiveness must be valid and reliable. Too often the cross-cultural worker does ministry but dismisses a lack of effectiveness to undefined intangibles that are assumed to be outside of one's control.

POSSIBLE ASSUMPTIONS OF CURRENT STORYTELLING APPROACHES

What are some of the possible underlying philosophical and theological assumptions of current storytelling approaches? We will explore five categories of assumptions. They are related to: (a) the Bible, (b) the role of the Holy Spirit, (c) time, (d) story methodology, and (e) the disciplines of language, culture, and worldview. See Figure 3.1. For each set of assumptions, we offer brief explanation and analyses of the underlying philosophy and theology.

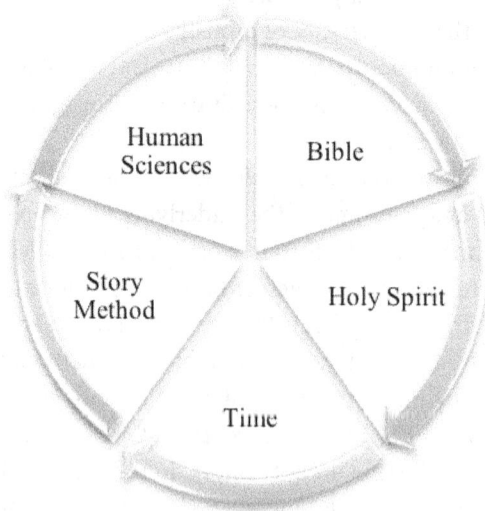

Figure 3.1: Five Grids of Analysis

Related to the Bible

Almost always out in the field when telling the biblical story across cultures, it is assumed that the Bible is unique . . . matchlessly powerful. It is different from all other literature. It will not fail. That is, if we attempt to communicate its content, we indeed will communicate and with power. This is the first and foremost assumption related to Bible storytelling in the global mission enterprise. It is common everywhere.

A corollary assumption, though less common, is that any amplification or exposition of the biblical story on the part of the teller is, at best, a distraction that lacks the inherent power of God's word and is therefore not needed.

So, the Bible is considered distinctively different from, say, Homer's *Iliad* and *Odyssey* or a list of ingredients on a box of Cheerios. It is able to accomplish purposes other literature is not. Perhaps it is not constrained by the science of rhetorical discourse. In support of these basic assumptions, C. S. Lewis writes, "The Bible is not merely a sacred book but a book so remorselessly and continuously sacred that it does not invite, it excludes or repels, the merely aesthetic approach".[12]

As we go further in this book, we will attempt to identify how the Bible is different than other literature but also how it is the same.

Continuing, here is a more specific assumption that is made about the Bible. Within the confines of Scripture, God has already addressed every core worldview presupposition of people in all cultures for all time. The stories themselves, unique because they are from the Bible, will address any worldview concern without the teller needing to previously know or concurrently confront those concerns. So, little to no exposition is required. Closely related is an assumption that simply telling the story will displace existing false presuppositions about what is and is not.

Put more strongly, the limited number of stories in the Bible represents God's preselected choices of communicable information that meets the needs of all people. John writes in his gospel that there is much more that could have been written about Jesus (John 21:25). Therefore, because

1. Lewis, *The Literary Impact of the Authorized Version*, 33.

2. Sayyid Qutb, an Egyptian-born Islamic theorist, speaks with similar adoration of the Qur'an: "The spring from which the Companions of the Prophet—peace be on him—drank was the Qur'an. The Holy Qur'an was the only source from which they quenched their thirst" (Qutb, Milestones, 16). Qutb says that Allah purified the Qur'an from the influence of all other sources (Ibid., 17).

so much more could have been written, what is written must be all that God supposes we need for communication and comprehension.[3]

What should we make of these assumptions? The human sciences have irrefutably established the complexity of humankind. Throughout this book there are repeated, although not exhaustive, explanations of that complexity and the difficulties associated with communication and change, both in allegiances to one's family and society as well as to worldview core assumptions.

Complexity of humankind relates to language as well as culture. Kathleen Callow addresses the enormity of the challenge to communicate effectively at the discourse level in her book *Man and Message: A Guide to Meaning-Based Text Analysis*. Callow analyzes how communication is structured to encode meaningful messages. Those structures vary across cultures. Consequently, the formation of meaning varies across cultures. Meaning is distilled from people's experiences in a given locale.[4] Strategic storytelling of the Bible would be required to understand those discourse processes and adapt methods across cultures.

Yet quick-fix cross-cultural methodologies still abound, by which an outsider enters a host society for a condensed period of time to share an abbreviated set of stories from Scripture. The simplicity of the approach does not fit the complexity of the need. It seems clear that such a simplistic approach is driven by an assumption that Scripture is uniquely powerful. So it comes as no surprise that J. O. Terry, an influential proponent of Bible storytelling, writes that telling the story of the Bible without exposition from the storyteller "implies a basic and simple trust in God's Word to be and do what it says it can do. It is powerful. It is Spirit inspired and Spirit illuminated".[5] Accordingly, he supports the sets of assumptions noted earlier. We do not, at least not in the way described above.

Again, to be clear, a screenwriter knows the requisite role of exposition in rhetorical discourse and worries to get it right.[6] The Alpha Workshop for Young Writers says, "The key thing here is to not think of your exposition as a separate thing from the story that needs to be imposed on the narrative, but as an organic part of it".[7] But, the biblical storyteller ar-

---

3. Miller, *Simply the Story Handbook*, 25.

4. Callow, *Man and Message*, 64.

5. Terry, *In Defense of Storying*, 1.

6. Wendig, *Exposition*, Terribleminds.com.

7. Brand, *The Four P's of Exposition*, Chronologicalbiblestorying.com.

gues that he does not need worry about exposition, presumably because the Bible is a different sort of narrative than those found in films. In the chapters that follow, however, we will show that the screenwriter and the biblical storyteller face an identical challenge in communicating effectively. In fact, the biblical storyteller's task is further compounded when working across cultures.[8]

Related to the Holy Spirit

A second category of assumptions relates to the Holy Spirit. A basic assumption may be something like this. The Holy Spirit will do the work of confronting and converting sinners. Additionally, as an unseen force, the Holy Spirit works to assuage false meaning, impart true biblical meaning, and produce expected outcomes. The following quote originates from leaders in the Orality Movement. We are not certain who wrote it. "Ultimate acceptance and retention of His story depends upon the work of the Holy Spirit as He places His story among the people as 'Holy Literature'".[9]

These possible assumptions related to the Holy Spirit may or may not be valid and reliable. Some may be but others may not. Is it possible that there is a "both/and" related to the Holy Spirit? To amplify, it indeed is the Holy Spirit who confronts and converts sinners. And, at the same time, the cross-cultural storyteller applies acquired understanding and skills related to intercultural communication. After all, in Acts 3 it was Peter who told the curious crowd that he was one of them as a fellow Israelites but it was they who killed the author of life (Acts 3:1–21). Why did he exploit shared identity? Why did he employ the literary device of rebuke?

Such divine and human collaboration is part of the whole biblical story from beginning to end. It may have started in creation when God bent down and breathed life into the newly created respiratory system of Adam. At once, life began and was sustained. Then, collaboration continued with the naming of the animals in the Garden of Eden. Throughout the Old Testament, God chose men and women to accomplish his purposes.

8. In Chapter 4 we will address the seeming confusion within the Orality Movement regarding the term *exposition*. Does the term refer to: (a) a preaching style where deliberate commentary explicitly wrings out all possible meanings from a Scriptural text or (b) a dramatic narrative device that unobtrusively includes background information necessary to understand the characters and plot of the story?

9. Authorship not stated, *A Methodology for Presenting the Gospel to Oral Communicators*, VII.6.

The mysteries of the virgin birth of the Lord Jesus Christ are illustrative and profound. Paul describes his own ministry with an agricultural metaphor where he plants, another waters, and God gives the increase.

In chapters to follow, we will circle back to these assumptions as we explore basic theories of communication and their application across cultures.

Related to Time

There are four salient assumptions related to time. They are:

- There is urgency to the Great Commission.

- Personnel can and should be deployed rapidly into cross-cultural contexts.

- The time-intensive, old-fashioned methods of culture and language acquisition are largely unnecessary because an urban or coastal national may be able to take the Gospel to the interior of a nation.

- Any set of biblical stories can be told swiftly, unlike expositional teaching, which tends to be protracted and delayed.[10]

We must ask and reflect carefully about the validity of these assumptions. In secular business among the private sector, empirical evidence has established that efficiency often compromises effectiveness (compare Drucker, 2006; also see Kettner, Moroney, & Martin, L., 2012 where the topic may be referenced as "benefit-cost analysis"). In the spiritual realm, however, when stories from the Bible are being shared, Christian workers too often strive only for efficiency, assuming the dynamics are different. The power of Scripture itself, they assume, combined with the inimitable ministry of the Holy Spirit offer a divine guarantee to effectiveness. Unlike

10. Note that some cultures dislike narrative brevity, as in the following analysis of ancient Indian epic storytelling: "The *Mahabharata* in fact shows few signs of hasty composition. Indeed, the overall narrative structure related by Vyasa's students Ugraśravas and Vaisampayana is remarkably paced and almost unbelievably patient. No listener rushes to skip the preliminaries in the desire to hear the heart of the story. Instead, the poem's various audiences actually hinder the poet's progress by never being satisfied with the rapid outlines of tales narrators occasionally offer. What satisfies is only the fullest account that gives every detail its due" (Christopher Strauss, 2009, a paper entitled *Vyasa's Oceanic Mind: An Approach to Reading the Mahabharata* submitted in the Mahabharata Preceptorial at St. John's College in Santa Fe, New Mexico).

a businessperson who must consider the benefit-cost ratio, the Bible story-teller is free to focus less on effectiveness. The storyteller is able to maximize efficiency. In other words, divinity relaxes the tension between effectiveness and efficiency if the story content is from the Bible. Efficiency is the prin-ciple task for human agency. Effectiveness is left to the divine. Of course, we could not disagree more.

Related to the Methodology of Story

Here are seven prominent assumptions related to storytelling:

- Storytelling is a powerful method of communication.

- Storytelling is layered on top of the efficacy of Scripture and omnipo-tence of the Holy Spirit.

- Storying is not confrontational. It is not preaching. It is not overt teaching. It is merely conveying the stories of God's Word and leaving the results to God. Most of the time, the hearers do not even realize that their values are changing. His word says that it will not return void or empty. So, the power of his word, combined with the power of the Holy Spirit, does amazing things.[11] "When you tell a story, you 'abduct' listeners from their known worlds into another world".[12]

- If biblical content is story-delivered, basic universals of interpretation are already embedded in the story method. Arduous past efforts to articulate the complicated processes of interpretation are not needed. Encoded meaning will be decoded correctly. "By simply learning a story, the basic tools of interpretation are already there".[13] J. O. Terry suggests that if biblical stories are accumulated, they will interpret themselves.[14] Exposition, an inherently weaker tool of rhetorical discourse, may thwart rather than enhance understanding.[15] Storying

11. Willis, *Making Disciples of Oral Learners*, 16.

12. Jones, *Postmodern Youth Ministry*, 27.

13. Jacobson, *Reading Response for Fiction*, 42.

14. Terry, *A Literate Walk Down an Oral Road*, 28.

15. Robert Kernen, the Emmy Award-winning author of *Building Better Plots* (1999), has a different view of exposition and story. He distinguishes exposition and narrative but does not feel they are in conflict. In his books, screenplays, and films, he "embroiders the tale with non-narrative details" naturally occurring within the telling of the story, such as character conversation and inner dialogue (personal correspondence April 23, 2009).

should have "no expositional content" (Learning Preference 10, CBS: A Methodology for Presenting the Gospel to Oral Communicators, 2001, p. I.20). This injunction is repeated throughout the Chronological Bible Storytelling instructional manual. Also, "Storying is self-correcting in that subsequent stories may correct misinterpretation in earlier stories as earlier stories give foundation for interpreting later stories thus preserving the wholeness of the message in the stories".[16]

- It is best to determine clarity at the end of uninterrupted storytelling.

- It may be helpful to clarify requisite biblical behavior, that is, what to do.

- People tell stories the same way. Therefore, almost anyone can enter a host society to share the Bible.

It is the integration of assumptions about the Bible, Holy Spirit, and methodology of story that has shut down the conversation. It is said the argument is over. The discussion has ended. Missiological history has run its course. We now know. Simply tell the story of the Bible trusting in the Holy Spirit. The integration of these three has become the triumvirate and trifecta.

And yet in this book series, we say there is more to the story. Out in the field, storytelling has not been a panacea, a cure-all. The needs are real and rampant. Evidence indicates storytelling is not a standalone approach. Storytelling must be embedded in a much broader holistic methodology of cross-cultural relationships and communication.

There is much more to come in subsequent chapters about story and storytelling in the cross-cultural context. Keep reading!

Related to Language, Culture, and Worldview

The following four assumptions have been emphasized related to language, culture, and worldview:

16. E. Ray Clendenen, Academic Editor at Boardman and Holman Publishers, comments on how language works in communication, especially the macrostructure of language. He understands that hortatory [exhortation] discourse works to effect behavioral change in the hearer. It exposes the situation in need of change. It motivates people to change by highlighting positives and negatives. It includes directives, crafted in culturally appropriate injunctions and exhortations. He sees Scripture as discourse seeking to create impact in the hearer and reader. Just like a story may have a climax, hortatory discourse has a change slot (2001). Compare this emphasis to 2 Corinthians 5:11, where Paul stated he worked hard to persuade others.

- The familiar regional trade language may be required and an acceptable vehicle for storytelling by an outsider. However, there is no longer a need for an expatriate to move interior to learn an indigenous language.

- Contextualization is only required as per language. Intentional cultural contextualization by the expatriate cross-cultural worker is not required.

- If locals retell the biblical story, they will naturally and tacitly take into account the culture of the new hearer. This assumption assumes the cultural gap of "locals" from locale to locale is small.

- Little to no culture or worldview investigation is required because the biblical stories automatically address all of elements therein.

Throughout the history of Christian expansion, cross-cultural workers have toiled with culture and language acquisition. This tradition is now coming into question. Largely influenced by previously assumptions related to the Bible, Holy Spirit, and methodology of story, the scientific disciples of culture and language have been set aside. Much more will be said about this in the chapters to follow.

CONCLUDING REFLECTIONS

The current practitioners of storytelling, whether they realize it or no, assume the following. There is a triumvirate foundation for effective communication across cultures: (a) the unparalleled efficacy of Scripture, (b) the omnipotence of the Holy Spirit, and (c) the natural power of narration in rhetorical discourse. This inimitable and inexorable triad yields unnatural results. The storyteller can concentrate on efficiency while God takes care of effectiveness. Even though global business leaders must wrestle with language and culture, the biblical storyteller, armed with Scripture and Spirit and story, need not.

If you were to reflect on the current approaches, what would be your analysis? What is clear? Would you concur that they have failed to fix the problems exposed in Chapter 2?

The chapter that follows introduces a solution.

PART TWO

Aiming for Clarity

4

Introducing a Solution

INTRODUCTORY REMARKS

CHAPTER 2 EXPOSED THE need by describing the complexities of ministry across cultures, alerting us that there is more we need to know about the enormity of the task. Chapter 3 analyzed the flawed assumptions of current approaches to storytelling, asking us if there are biblical and scientific foundations for them. Here in Chapter 4 we introduce a possible solution. One may ask, "A solution to what problem?" To be as specific as possible, missiologist Paul Hiebert describes the problem as Christo-paganism, an avertable aftermath of cross-cultural ministry. He laments that people across cultures often add Christianity as a new layer of belief and practice on top of old ways of living. Adding something new does not necessarily supplant what is old.

In *Understanding Folk Religion*, Hiebert and his coauthors describe this syncretism as the "uneasy coexistence of Christianity and paganism".[1] They argue that the syncretism is occurring all over the world and creating havoc in churches. "An uncritical incorporation of old beliefs and practices in the life of the church opens the door to syncretism of all kinds as well as to cultural and philosophical relativism, which destroys all truth and authority".[2][3]

---

1. Hiebert et al., *Understanding Folk Religion*, 19.

2. Ibid., 21.

3. In the quote cited above, Hiebert claims *all* truth and authority are destroyed by relativism. This is true in an absolute sense in the abstract, but is not true in the geographic contexts we presented in Chapter 2. Yes, syncretism is a form of relativism that causes grave problems for biblical truth and authority. But locals in these regions strongly submit to "truth" as they know it phenomenologically as well as particularistic authorities. In fact,

This series, book, and chapter argue that syncretism can be minimized through a more comprehensive approach to cross-cultural ministry. Through a twelve-part methodology, this comprehensive approach exploits the effectiveness of story and does not neglect the power of worldview. It understands the tenacity of core worldview assumptions and asserts that they must be unmistakably confronted in a context of genuine relationships. The methodology integrates cultural anthropology and theology.[4]

Before describing the twelve steps, it may be helpful to lay a foundation for understanding the proposed methodology. We will first examine the concept of *worldview*. Then, we will define *symbols* and show how they work in the "lived experience" of individuals and a society's "conscience collective".[5]

WORLDVIEWS

Definition of Worldview

What is worldview? It is the story-based grid through which one "sees" and interprets all aspects of life. Worldview is inseparably linked to symbol and story.[6] It is a present tense grid, synchronic, or at a point in time.[7] Metanarrative, on the other hand, is diachronic, or a big picture story that develops, unfolds, and spans across time. The grid of worldview is not only story-based, but it also contains integrated components.

---

this dual allegiance is part of the problem. Hiebert also combines cultural and philosophical relativism as if they are synonymous. They are not. Cultural relativism in some regards is a positive mindset. Philosophical relativism for the follower of Christ is not.

4. Davies, *Anthropology and Theology*.

5. Dilthey, *The Formation of the Historical World in the Human Sciences*. See also Durkheim, *Selected Writings*.

6. How does story tie to worldview? Research by the Hugh Downs School of Human Communication at Arizona State University (ASU) explains how "master narratives" knit together to form a "rhetorical vision" (Halverson et al., *Master Narratives*). The ASU researchers studied master narratives of Islamic extremism that recur globally. Based on the story plots, repeated characters, and themes, these master narratives inform a common worldview among some people.

7. Hiebert et al., *Understanding Folk Religion*, 31.

Components of Worldview

The story grid of worldview has components that are universal to people. Michael Kearney, a social researcher in Mexico and professor at the University of California, sees worldview in six separate but interrelated classifications: self, Other, relationships, causality, time, and space.[89] He argues that a worldview in any culture may be classified according to these core assumptions.

Kearney builds the system of worldview classifications on the tradition of Robert Redfield and others. Redfield (1953) asserts, "Self is the axis of worldview".[10] *Self* defines itself in relationship to *Other*. Within the *relationship* between self and Other is *causality* or agency, all of which is played out on the stage of life in *time* and *space*.

Worldview and culture are not synonyms. Culture is the learned and shared patterns of perception and behavior. Worldview is one of the layers of culture. Redfield says worldview "is the way a people characteristically look outward upon the universe".[11]

Location of Worldview in the Model of Culture

The worldview grid of core assumptions about what is and is not real is at the epicenter of culture. To capture this, Global Perspective Consulting (GPC) designed a model of culture that locates worldview below the

8. Kearney, *World View*, 106.

9. Worldview Resource Group provides definitions of the six classifications: (a) *Self* is the entire essential entity of a sentient human being who is distinct from but able to dynamically relate to Other. (b) *Other* is the total environment that is distinct from but related to self. Other includes the material and immaterial worlds, entities that are otherworldly and this worldly, including human and nonhumans. (c) *Relationship* is the dynamic value-based interaction between self and Other that occurs within socio-cultural institutions. (d) *Causality* is the orderly structured interplay between causes and effects. (e) *Time* is a past, present, and future sequence of existence and events. (f) *Space* is a demarcated multi-dimensional realm in which all things exist and all events occur. Time and space occasionally rise to a level beyond simply the stage of life. They both can become foils in the story. For example, time is elevated to a place of causality among people who see time as linear and segment it into measurable and scheduled components such as minutes, hours, and days. A time/task orientation becomes a story character that influences the movement of the life story. In a similar way, space can rise to a role of causality. Some people believe that a confluence of spiritual powers may occupy a territorial region. Or, societies understand that designated locations are sacred.

10. Redfield, *The Primitive Worldview and Its Transformations*, 91.

11. Redfield, *The Primitive Worldview and Its Transformations*, 85.

surface, almost always invisible, most often tacitly assumed, and powerful in that it impacts every aspect of life.

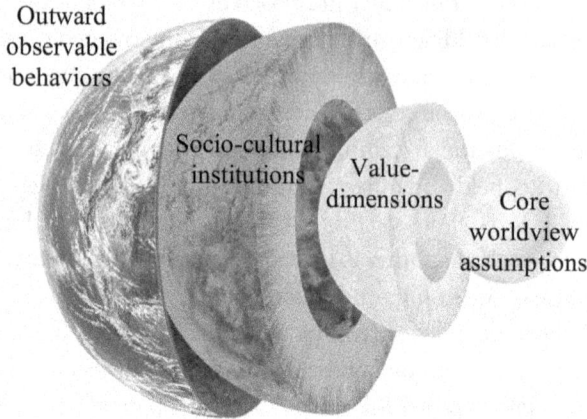

Outward
observable
behaviors

Socio-cultural
institutions

Value-
dimensions

Core
worldview
assumptions

Figure 4.1: Model of Culture

Figure 4.1[12] uses the organic metaphor of earth to represent how culture functions across its layers. The outward observable behaviors are like the crust of the earth. Seismologists suggest that we can understand how thin the earth's crust is by thinking of an apple's skin. On average the earth's crust is only five kilometers thick. Culture is similar. What we say and do represent only a fraction of what makes up the whole of our culture.

Below the surface is a mantle of socio-cultural institutions that promotes and prohibits behavior. It represents the way a group of people formalizes and codifies their standards and morals. Institutions include family, religion, government, judicial systems, law enforcement, and more.

Beneath the institutions of culture are value-dimensions at the outer core layer. Often represented by pairs, such as "individualism and collectivism", these values impact what we feel ought and ought not to be done and said. At the center of culture, at its inner core, are basic worldview assumptions about reality. About what is and is not.

12. Image credit: Gary Hincks/Science Photo Library

Characteristics of Worldview

Such fundamental and underlying expectations of worldview are deeply embedded in the mind, emotions, and identity of people. Though invisible, they are emotionally embraced. They generally remain outside of one's awareness, and therefore are tacitly assumed.

Core worldview assumptions change neither quickly nor easily. Why? The metanarrative foundation that informs this rhetorical vision is historical, venerable, and deemed reliable by people. Arizona State University (ASU) researchers write that a *master narrative* is "a transhistorical narrative that is deeply embedded in a particular culture".[13] These controlling stories are widely shared and repeated across time. Based upon the resulting worldview, people in a culture conceive of themselves in terms of these stories, which configure life events into a coherent theme. People project the future as a continuation of a metanarrative.[14]

Hiebert and colleagues write that worldviews are fundamental givens with which people in a community think, not what they think about. Because worldview assumptions are taken for granted, they are largely unexamined and implicit. They are reinforced by deep feelings. Anyone who challenges them challenges the very foundations of people's lives.[15]

If the research by ASU is valid and if Hiebert and colleagues are right, the role and function of worldview in a culture profoundly and strategically impact storytelling. If the storyteller understood the impact of worldview, one would not share mere story bits after abruptly entering a cultural society.

Kearney goes on to define the basic concepts related to worldview.[16] He characterizes worldview as:

- The way people look at reality and think about the world (more or less coherent, though not necessarily accurate)

- An integrated collection of basic, first-order assumptions and images[17]

13. Halverson et al., *Master Narratives*, 14.

14. Ibid., 181–82.

15. Hiebert et al., *Understanding Folk Religion*, 40.

16. Kearney, *World View*, 41.

17. This collection of basic assumptions and images is different from stated beliefs, that is, if a person is able to say, "I believe . . . " then that postulation is a *result* of worldview not the worldview itself (Needham, *Belief, Language, and Experience*). "A worldview is not merely a philosophical by-product of each culture, like a shadow, but the very

- A cognitive phenomenological framework, structure, or schemata
- Culturally organized macrothought

He sees worldview as a system. Each component fits into the whole. Each is interrelated and interdependent. Everything is inextricably linked.[18]

Implications of a Worldview Approach to Ministry

A dilemma facing the cross-cultural worker today is that worldview seems too complicated to consider. It *is* complicated. But the truth of the matter is that it is too important to ignore.[19] Just as a medical doctor would not treat a physical malady without first understanding what it is, the cross-cultural worker should not address outward observable behaviors without correspondingly attending to the socio-cultural institutions that promote such behaviors as well as exposing the value-dimensions deep beneath the surface of culture from which the behaviors are derived. Furthermore, authentic and sustained change would not take place unless the cross-cultural worker skillfully challenged the core worldview assumptions underlying culture and from which all is derived. The problem of a multi-tiered Christianity with its devastating and debilitating syncretism is solved through worldview change. If worldview is not addressed, of a surety, Christo-paganism will result. And, this is what is taking place as described in Chapter 2.

---

skeleton of concrete cognitive assumptions on which the flesh of customary behavior is hung. Worldview, accordingly, may be expressed, more or less systematically, in cosmology, philosophy, ethics, religious ritual, scientific belief, and so on, but it is implicit in almost every act" (Wallace, *Culture and* Personality, 143).

18. Ludwig van Bertalanffy saw similar systems in his biology research (Bertalanffy, *General System Theory*). A medical doctor uses systems thinking and practice to diagnose and treat a patient's disease. When our family saw a drooping on the left side of my father's face, he was not treated by an occupational therapist to restore his smile. A team of physicians traced the connection between the drooping in his cheek to his trigeminal cranial nerve. The sheath of the nerve revealed metastasized cancer cells that were ultimately sourced to adenoid cystic carcinoma in his frontal sinus cavity. Ensuing treatment included surgery, chemotherapy, exercise, and diet. Systems thinking and practice also applies to worldview.

19. Too complicated to consider . . . too important to ignore.

Transformation of a Worldview

Again, Hiebert helps us understand the magnitude of worldview transformation. In his model, a worldview is comprised of a synchronic map of themes, counterthemes, symbolic metaphors, and foundations, each of which and all of which must be transformed.[20] See Figure 4.2. If what Hiebert and others in the sociological and anthropological fields are saying is true, then the task of worldview change is mammoth. Truly, man is fearfully and wonderfully made (Psalm 139:14). On the whole, there is incredible complexity. The old ways are entrenched and often seemingly intractable.[21]

A hopeful yet unbiblical and unscientific assumption is that God mysteriously displaces this synchronic map that Hiebert deftly describes. If that assumption is correct, this book is completely unnecessary. Of course, the authors of the book series do not share that assumption. In fact, it appears absurd to suggest that tweets, email blasts, or story bits are viable approaches to cross-cultural ministry and worldview displacement. Don Kirkpatrick, communication expert, past President of the American Society for Training and Development, and a senior elder at Elmbrook Church in Brookfield, Wisconsin, argues that effective communication is 100 percent the responsibility of the sender.[22] The sender must skillfully mediate the encoded message.

20. Hiebert, *Transforming Worldviews*, 335.

21. See Strauss, Robert, and Tom Steffen. "Change the Worldview . . . Change the World." *Evangelical Missions Quarterly* 45 (2009) 458–64.

22. Kirkpatrick, *No-Nonsense Communication*, 41.

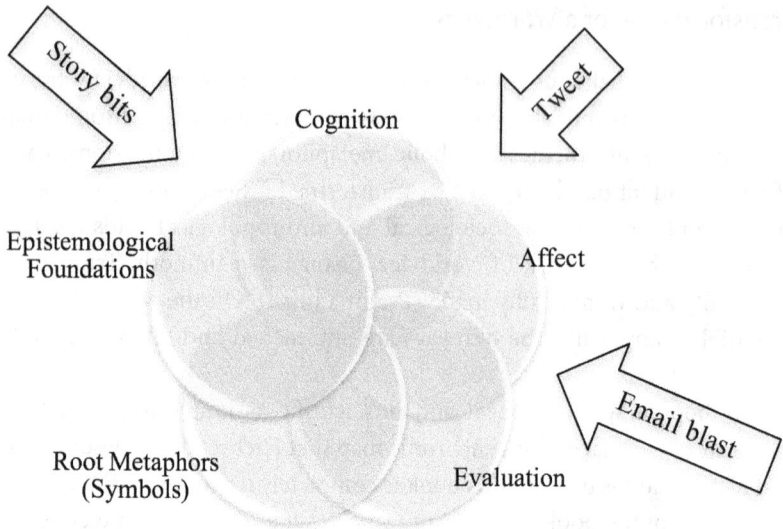

Figure 4.2: Hiebert Synchronic Map

SYMBOLS

Definition of Symbol

The foundation of human behavior is the ability to create and use symbols.[23] Leslie White, an American anthropologist, argues, "All human behavior consists of, or is dependent upon, the use of symbols . . . all culture (civilization) depends upon the symbol".[24] He defines a symbol as "a thing the value or meaning of which is bestowed upon it by those who use it".[25] White uses the term "thing" because a symbol can take on any form: odor, sound, color, taste, objects, and so forth.[26]

---

23. See Steffen, Tom. "Foundational Roles of Symbol and Narrative in the (Re)construction of Reality and Relationship." *Missiology: An International Review* 26 (1998) 477–94.

24. White, *The Science of Culture*, 22, 33.

25. Ibid., 25.

26. We define the term *symbol* more generically than the *Handbook of Literary Terms* (2005). Kennedy, Gioia, and Bauerlein say that symbol is a person, place, or thing but its meaning goes beyond a literal sense (Kennedy et al., *Handbook of Literary Terms*, 148). Hiebert sees this distinction and calls these transcendent signs *nondiscursive symbols* (Hiebert et al., *Understanding Folk Religions*, 244).

Function of Symbols

Inseparably connected to stories, symbols provide the foundation of all human behavior and communication. Clifford Geertz, proponent of symbolic anthropology, (see also Douglas, *Natural Symbols* and Turner, *Dramas, Fields, and Metaphors*) argues that culture "denotes an historically transmitted pattern of meanings embodied in symbols, a system of inherited conceptions expressed in symbolic forms by means of which men communicate, perpetuate, and develop their knowledge about and attitudes toward life".[27]

When constructed into systems, symbols reflect our underlying assumptions. They are accepted without question. Through a shared symbol system, people ask questions, share experiences, interpret reality and relationships, and tell stories. It is through storytelling that the meanings of symbols are refined and revised.

STRATEGIC STORYTELLING

Story is a stylized communication pattern of symbols with pictures in the mind transferred to others so that awe and imagination take center stage, accenting cognition and volition. Story uses culturally shared symbols communicated through context-specific schema. How symbol and story come together is fundamental to one's being able to participate in culture.

Symbols, to be truly symbolic culturally, sooner or later find themselves embedded in story. For followers of Christ, the cup and the bread perpetuate symbolic meaning because of two basic narratives, the Passover and the death and resurrection of Jesus. The same is true of facts. To be truly factual, they require a story. Trials are much more than evidence and "convincing facts." They offer story lines developed by lawyers who not only bias their client, but also hopefully seem credible to the life stories of the judge or jurors. Convincing lawyers narrate the facts in a logical pattern that fits the mindset of the judge or jurors.

Theories are much more than abstract constructs. They are, in reality, finely honed stories that represent a particular view of the world. When a theory becomes obsolete, it becomes a discarded story. Likewise, logic and systemization bear similarities to stories. Psychologist George Howard writes, "Logic or rationality represents a type of story (or kind of analysis)

---

27. Geertz, *The Interpretation of Cultures*, 89.

that one might choose to apply to a particular problem (or situation) in order to understand the issues at stake and discover plans of action that one might entertain".[28]

Anthropology, as any discipline, has its dumpsite for challenged theories. The first anthropological missiologists, such as Thomas and Elizabeth Brewster, Paul Hiebert, Charles Kraft, Marvin Mayers, Lyman Reed, and Alan Tippett, were influenced strongly by the theory of structural functionalism.[29] Today, the limits of this explanatory theory of cultural change and human behavior are more widely recognized and challenged (for the moment) by competing stories, such as conflict theory, cultural materialism (maximizing local resources), or social biology (survival).

Theology, like anthropology, comes in meta-stories, backed by certain biblical theories. The meta-stories (sacred stories) of dispensationalism, covenant theology, black theology, Liberation Theology, water buffalo theology, and a host of others serve as the backdrop to interpret those seemingly contradictory verses or to challenge or reconcile outside perspectives (competing stories). The theologies (stories) that have the "ring of truth" tend to be those that reflect the meta-story of the specific theology.

Constructivist psychologist Miller Mair astutely points out the role of story in worldview, whether through facts, theories, logic, or systemizations:

> Stories are habitations. We live in and through stories. They conjure worlds. We do not know the world other than as story world. Stories inform life. They hold us together and keep us apart. We inhabit the great stories of our culture. We live through stories. We are *lived* by the stories of our race and place. It is this enveloping and constituting function of stories that is especially important to sense more fully. We are, each of us, locations where the stories of our place and time become partially tellable.[30]

Due to the pervasive, primal nature of symbol-based story in the (re)construction of perceived reality and competing realities, humans rely heavily, and usually unconsciously, on this genre in numerous ways. Georgetown University professor Barbara Harding captures the broad-sweeping nature of narrative: "We dream in narrative, daydream in narrative, remember, anticipate, hope, despair, believe, doubt, plan, revise,

---

28. Howard, *A Narrative Approach to Thinking*, 189.

29. Steffen, *Passing the Baton*, 142–43.

30. Mair, "Psychology as Storytelling," 127.

criticize, gossip, learn, hate, and love by narrative".[31] Missiologist David J. Hesselgrave demonstrates the role of narrative in the origin story (what the Romanian historian Mircea Eliade calls *cosmogonic myth*[32]) of different societies. Note also the symbols.

> The truth of the matter is that narrative has been the mode by which worldviews have been transmitted and understood by the people of almost all cultures all down through history. Hindus have their stories of Brahmananda and the World Egg. The Chinese have the story of Pan-Ku, the original man whose body parts became the mountains, plains, and rivers of China. The Japanese have the story of Izanagi and Izanami whose playful time on the "bridge of heaven" resulted in the formation of the Japanese archipelago. Naturalistic evolutionists have their story of the rise of life from the primordial mists of eons past.[33]

Story is much more than an art form, entertainment, or literary genre; it is a way to structure thought.[34] We are not only what we eat; we are also what we "symbol" and "story."

A METHODOLOGY FOR STRATEGIC STORYTELLING

Given the imperative to carry out ministry in the cross-cultural setting at a worldview level, we propose a methodology for *strategic storytelling*. There is a chronology to the method with starting and ending points. There is a procedure to the method.

The methodology includes twelve steps that are carried out systematically based upon underlying assumptions. Those underlying philosophical and theological assumptions are analyzed in Chapter 9. Here is a list and brief description of the twelve steps, shared in the vernacular of story. Each step will be expanded in more detail in Chapters 6–8:

1. *Investigate the cultural storylands* through existing academic literature. There are three storylands to investigate. The research can commonly be done prior to entering the host society. For example, there are over 5,000 volumes addressing the cultures of First Nations people

---

31. Harding, "Towards a Poetic of Fiction," 5.

32. Eliade, "Cosmogonic Myth and 'Sacred History,'" 171–83.

33. Hesselgrave, "Christian Contextualization and Biblical Theology," 28.

34. Bradt, *Story as a Way of Knowing*.

of North America catalogued in the Murray Library of the University of Saskatchewan in Saskatoon, Canada.

What are the three storylands?

    a. The culture of the biblical story: Scripture is made clear by understanding the culture of the Ancient Near East.

    b. The culture of the cross-cultural worker: The starting point for all intercultural communication is first understanding oneself.

    c. The culture of the host society: Anthropological tools are essential to effectiveness across cultures.

2. *Enter the story* of the host society by establishing authentic relationships. There is absolutely no substitute for a "being among the people" approach to cross-cultural ministry.[35] Effectiveness demands immersion. It requires firsthand experience living in the setting among people. Culture and language acquisition are non-optional. Worldview storytelling will be hard work. It is said that Thomas Edison quipped, "Opportunity is missed by most people because it is dressed in overalls and looks like work". A team may consist of both short-and long-term participants depending on roles and responsibilities.

3. *Model the story* in keeping with the historic traditions of both Christianity and Islam where the "messenger" takes precedence over the "message". Kirkpatrick says rapport, which he defines as "attitudes, feelings, and relationships between sender and receiver", is the number one ingredient for effective communication.[36] Modeling at this early stage in the methodology may only be elementary, with behavior

35. The authors are fully aware of rebuttals to an incarnational approach, rebuttals that argue that the Holy Spirit carries out the work of the ministry as He builds up a church in Christ. Such rebuttals assert that it is the presence of the Holy Spirit that is requisite, not the presence of the cross-cultural worker. Additionally, some assert that the term *incarnational* has not been operationally defined, therefore cross-cultural workers are confused as to the degree of contextualization that is required to meet a standard of incarnation. For a statement of these assertions, see J. Todd Billings' *Union with Christ: Reframing Theology and Ministry for the Church*. What are the operational differences between an incarnational approach and missional contextualization? In what ways was John Stott not enlightened as he reasoned from John 20:21? Rebutting Stott, Andreas Kostenburger asks, "Moreover, if Jesus' incarnation is to function as the model for the church's mission, why not Jesus' provision of atonement?" (Kostenburger, *The Missions of Jesus*, 216). Is such a question really valid?

36. Kirkpatrick, *No-Nonsense Communication*, 44.

informed through investigations from Step 1. Modeling is a value that characterizes all steps.

4. *Collect symbols and stories* (based upon gender, geography, and generations). To effectively understand people in the host society, the cross-cultural worker collects symbols and stories across broad spectrums. This step extends Step 1 and is carried out on site.

5. *Analyze stories* to determine how they make meaning. In what ways do local stories create meaning? What is that meaning? What are the socio-cultural institutions? In what ways will the rival biblical metanarrative confront and disrupt the form and function of social organization, political organization, economic exchange, and other structures? Therefore, what remedies does God provide? What deep value-dimensions drive observable behaviors? What core worldview assumptions determine perception about what is and is not real?

6. *Understand local metanarrative* and the resulting worldview as a basis for communication.

7. *Communicate the biblical story* with targeted symbol-based content. It is imperative to think in terms of whole-to-part rather than merely sharing "story bits". Worldview change is the outcome of metanarrative rivalry.

8. *Internalize the biblical story* to facilitate extemporaneous delivery and authenticate legitimacy.

9. *Tell to teach* (*t2T*) the biblical story by means of localized forms and functions. Strategic storytelling is predicated upon the assumption that simply using a symbol or telling a story is ineffectual. The ultimate objective is not to simply tell (*t* . . .) but to teach (. . . 2T) or cause to learn.

10. *Validate meaning* through feedback by means of symbol and story solicitation with key term verification. Careful attention in the validation process must be paid to power distance, shame, honor, and face-saving. Respondents may or may not be able to respectfully share what they do or do not understanding.

11. *Train new symbol observers and storytellers*. Cross-cultural ministry requires not simply evangelism but discipleship–creating authentic followers of God built up in Christ in a community of faith and functioning missionally in their local context and beyond.

12. *Reach the storylands.* The ultimate goal of ministry is that men, women, and children worldwide have had a valid opportunity to enter into a relationship with God, wherein they enjoy and glorify Him in the midst of a community of faith.

CONCLUDING REFLECTIONS

What have we said in this chapter? Building on Chapters 2 and 3, there is a problem with syncretism in cross-cultural ministry. In other words, a person's heart allegiances and frame of reference are not being transformed by quick or piecemeal story approaches. Our suspicion . . . no, our conclusion based on research is that worldview is not being adequately addressed. Why? Perhaps we do not understand fully enough what worldview is and how it works. The chapter took time to explore worldview in greater depth.

We introduced the phenomena of symbols as a starting point in worldview exploration. Then, the chapter provided a brief overview of the strategic storytelling methodology that the book offers as a solution to the malady of rampant syncretism.

In the chapters that follow, we will provide much more detail about each of the twelve steps in the methodology.

5

Making the Case for Strategic Storytelling

"God made man because he loves stories."

—Elie Wiesel

INTRODUCTORY REMARKS

Stories are "more true" than facts because they are multidimensional.[1] Facts are like empty burlap sacks, unable to stand upright. Stories provide a context for inert facts, infusing them with life and meaning. It may be that facts will not persuade someone, but stories will "awaken sleeping wisdom".[2] Stories leverage the polarities of reason and emotion. A Jewish teaching story goes like this:

> Truth, naked and cold, had been turned away from every door in the village. Her nakedness frightened the people. When Parable found her she was huddled in a corner, shivering and hungry. Taking pity on her, Parable gathered her up and took her home. There, she dressed Truth in story, warmed her and sent her out again. Clothed in story, Truth knocked again at the villagers' doors and was readily welcomed into the people's houses. They invited her to eat at their table and warm herself by their fire.

---

1. Simmons, *The Story Factor*, 33.
2. Ibid., 50.

Story is the literary device that provides the best opportunity for giving birth to faith. But it does not do so automatically. Storytelling must be strategic.

When your story becomes my story, then you have converted me. Once my story changes, then I will change my behavior. This more closely represents authentic, sustained transformation. If I change my behavior without changing my story, I merely conform. When the pressure is off, I will revert to who I truly am.[3] "The truths of stories are made, not by logical persuasion, but by experiential engagement. Stories do not convince by argument; they surprise by identification".[4]

So, this chapter tells the story of what story is and what it does. The authors rely on scholarship from broad and varied disciplines. For several who may be well read in precedent literature about storytelling, some descriptions may be review. For many, though, there will be fresh, thought-provoking insights as we make the case for strategic storytelling, an approach that embeds storytelling in a broader holistic methodology of cross-cultural ministry.

WHAT STORY IS

To define story, I would like to tell about a real world experience.

"As someone pressed his hand into my lower back, the pain was excruciating. My breath was short. I could hear shouting in the *Da'an* language, but I couldn't understand a word of what was being said. Behind me a *Da'an* man was trying to hold me in a seated position. In front of me was a massive fallen tree with Rotan vines intermingled in the branches. To my right on the ground was my father's 35 mm Canon AE-1 camera. I had been taking pictures of *Da'an* men clearing the jungle for a rice garden.

From underneath the foliage of the tree I could hear my brother-in-law Ken, "I don't want to die!" Again he screamed, "I don't want to die!" I tried to stand up. I didn't know what happened. I couldn't remember anything. As soon as I got to my feet, I fell forward on my face, not able to keep my balance or endure the pain in my back and ribs.

Again I regained consciousness. The *Da'an* men had hastily made two stretchers from the smaller branches, tied together with fresh, stripped bark. I learned later that Ken had explained to them how to make the stretchers,

---

3. Walter Ong (2002) refers to this process (what the theologian may call transformation) as *interiorization*.

4. Shaw, *Storytelling in Religious Education*, 61.

as he had been retrieved from underneath the foliage. Ken spoke the *Da'an* language after three years of study and with his wife Cindy had lived in the jungle village of Nanga Raun for the past five years. Later I also learned that the owner of the rice garden land had fled into the jungle and would not reappear for three days for fear of reprisal from our families. The mountain on which we were injured was on the Island of Kalimantan.

Without straps to hold us securely onto the stretchers and in reckless haste, the carriers dashed down the mountain. We bounced up and down, both of us screaming in agony. The pace was frantic as the *Da'an* people were in a panic. The airstrip and Ken's house were only twenty minutes below, but the descent seemed like hours. We arrived still alive, but had completed only one part of a multi-leg journey toward medical help. We did not know it at the time, but it would be the following day before we would arrive at the Bethesda Medical Mission Hospital in Serukam.

I was told several months later that the tree that had fallen on Ken and me was almost one hundred feet tall and four feet wide at its base! We were severely injured. We were hours from any professional medical services, deep in the jungle of West Kalimantan.

Carole and I had come to Indonesia to spend a summer doing field-work. This was our first trip to Indonesia. Now I was fighting for my life . . . "

WHAT STORY DOES[5]

Story is a Way of Knowing

The above story is true. It happened in the summer of 1984. The events were life changing and although I do not remember being hit by the tree, I

---

5. This list identifies the eleven subheadings that follow under "What story does?" in Chapter 5. They pinpoint the functional activities of story.
1. A way of knowing
2. Evokes emotion
3. Builds off of experience
4. Draws in listeners
5. Constructs identity
6. Provides a comprehensive whole
7. Simplifies a cosmology
8. Speaks metaphorically
9. Combine to create a larger narrative
10. Can be divided into component parts
11. Provides a universal medium

will never forget the experiences of that summer years ago. They are relived in the retelling of the story. "Story and experience thus mix together and comingle in the storying process leaving indelible traces with each other so that neither story nor experience can be known again without memories and associations of the other".[6]

Kevin Bradt, a psychotherapist from Berkeley, California, asks, "Which do we know is real, the actual experience or the story we tell?" He argues that story is a way of knowing. Old Testament scholar Walter Brueggemann writes that story is "our primal and most characteristic mode of knowledge.[78]

All I consciously know about the events on the island of Kalimantan in the summer of 1984, I know through the story I now tell. For me, the story is reality.[9] This book presents story as an epistemology or a way of knowing. Helen Keller, blind, deaf, and mute from an illness at the age of 18 months, as an adult and educator described her wordless early world as an "unconscious, yet conscious time of nothingness. I did not know that I knew aught, or that I lived or acted or desired".[10] Wordless, storyless, no way of knowing . . .

Story Evokes Emotion

I've told the tree story many times since 1984. Throughout the story the gracious providence of God is evident. Even now tears fill my eyes as I write these words and relive the events. Not only is story a way of knowing, but also the memory and retelling of the story stir up deep feelings. The nature of story goes beyond cognitive reasoning or the intellect. It evokes emotion.

---

6. Bradt, *Story as a Way of Knowing*, 14. See also Wright, *The New Testament and the People of God*, 45.

7. Brueggemann, *The Creative Word*, 23.

8. Earlier, Claude Levi-Strauss posits that the story form reflects the fundamental structure of our minds (Levi-Strauss, *The Savage Mind*). Peter Berger suggests, "existentialist presuppositions can be posited as basic features of the human condition" (Berger, *The Sacred Canopy*, 167; see also Wright, *The New Testament and the People of God*, 38).

9. The term *noise* refers to "any element that interferes with the generation of the intended meaning in the mind of the receiver. Messages invariably produce responses, but the responses are far from perfectly predictable. The noise within the receiver . . . will determine to a great extent what the receiver will perceive" (McCroskey, *An Introduction to Rhetorical Communication*, 9–10.

10. Lamb, *The Art and Craft of Storytelling*, 6.

Annette Simmons says the difference between giving an example and telling a story is the addition of emotion.[11]

Story has the ability to make one hopeful, uncomfortable, angry, happy, sad, and empathetic—spanning the entire spectrum of human feeling. A profoundly meaningful experience with its associated images and emotions always results in a story. Fiction author Ruth Sawyer writes that above everything else the urgency behind a story is an experience that has deeply moved the storyteller.[12]

"The deepest convictions of our heart are formed by stories and reside there in the images and emotions of story".[13] Ossie Davis, an American playwright, says, "But it was to storytelling that I ran, as fast as I could, laughing in advance at the thought of the pleasure and surprise that was surely waiting for me".[14] Later we will return to the topic of emotion to emphasize its role in true learning.

Story Builds off of Experience

There is an ever-present reciprocity between experience and story. "But why story and why storytelling? Story is a primary language of experience.[15] Telling and listening to a story have the same structure as our experience".[16] Experience is best represented and more closely resembled by story.[17] Recounting the tree experience in Indonesia by making a list or creating an outline would hardly capture the traumatic reality of the events that took place in the sultry jungle on that stifling summer afternoon.

Addressing the best approach to learning, David Kolb writes, "The most effective type of learning—that which is most likely to influence attitudes and behavior—comes through having emotionally involving

11. Simmons, *The Story Factor*, 31.

12. Sawyer, *The Way of the Storyteller*, 28. She is referring to a deep feeling within the storyteller not to an abrupt blurting.

13. Curtis and Eldridge, *The Sacred Romance*, 38.

14. Goss and Goss, *Jump and Say!*, 19.

15. "According to the gospel taught by the missionaries, in heaven Christian Indians will be separated from our pagan ancestors and will live for eternity in a world ("new heaven and new earth") populated primary by our conquerors and colonizers (George E. "Tink" Tinker in *A Native American Theology*, 71).

16. Boomershine, *Story Journey*, 18.

17. Curtis and Eldridge, *The Sacred Romance*, 38; see also Wright, *The New Testament and the People of God*, 39.

experiences and reflecting upon them".[18] Almost always, reflection takes the form of story. Kolb's model of experiential learning is based on the work of John Dewey who sees experience as inseparable from learning—"an intimate and necessary relation".[19]

In his incomparable analysis of the Sacred Scriptures, Leland Ryken states, "The power of story as a literary form is its uncanny ability to involve us in what is happening. Look upon biblical stories as an invitation to share an experience, as vividly and concretely as possible, with the characters in the story".[2021] John Dominic Crossan, a New Testament scholar, writes, "We live in story like fish in the sea".[22]

Story Draws in Listeners

Whether my story or an account from the biblical narrative, those who listen are pulled into the story. Simmons says that bribery is a push strategy, but story is a pull strategy.[23] Stories influence through a process of drawing in the hearer, causing one to feel as though he is actually in the story rather than just hearing about it or observing the action as a distant spectator.[24]

"The most powerful narcotic in the world is the promise of belonging".[25] Author Kurt Bruner writes, "There is an epic drama unfolding on the stage of time. You and I are part of the cast. The play is written and directed by the Almighty himself. Every line, every scene, every twist, and every turn will culminate in the most amazing and satisfying conclusion ever performed".[26] You and I are in the Playwright's story. And it is the story that tells us who we are.

---

18. Kolb, *Experiential Learning*, 59.

19. Dewey, *Experience & Education*, 20.

20. Ryken, *How to Read the Bible as Literature*, 34–35.

21. *The Book of God: The Bible as a Novel* by Walter Wangerin, Jr. (1996, Zondervan) is considered the magnum opus of the well-known author. The book illustrates the story nature of the Bible where history and fact take on personality and warmth (front flap of dust cover).

22. Crossan, *The Dark Interval*, 47.

23. Simmons, *The Story Factor*, 108.

24. Fackre, "Christ's Ministry and Ours," 59.

25. Lasn, *Culture Jam*, xiii.

26. Bruner, K., *The Divine Drama*, ix.

Story Constructs Identity

"It is only in the narrative mode that one can construct an identity".[27] If I know the story of which I am part, I can answer the questions, 'Who am I?' and 'What am I to do?'.[28] It has been said that not only are we made in the image of God, but we are also made in the image of the story we have heard and told. Paul Ricoeur says it this way, "Individual and community are constituted in their identity by taking up narratives that become for them their actual history . . . subjects recognize themselves in the stories they tell about themselves".[29]

If a story is not told or if it dies, you and I may not remember who we are and why we are here.[30] Accordingly, sustained transformation in an individual or society requires old stories be replaced with new ones. This is the secret to ministry in cross-cultural settings.

Why is this so? The story form is the construct that informs our worldview function. Worldview is a culmination of the common story from which a community derives common sense. In a community, the common story is more than just shared; it is authoritative and canonized in a foundational role of the construction of reality and relationships.[31]

Story Provides a Comprehensive Whole

Prolific writer Nancy Lamb suggests that "story provides the building blocks for peace; it has forecast dangers, vilified enemies, and celebrated heroes".[32] Grant Wiggins and Jay McTighe capture the secret to a story's power. They argue that the influence of story is in the conflict and resolution, the rhythm of expectation and satisfaction.[33]

A good story in Western cultures delays the answer, thus creating the mystery and dilemma, piquing our interest. By weaving together the setting,

27. Bruner, J., *The Culture of Education*, 42. See also Hauerwas, *A Community of Character*, 9–35.

28. MacIntyre, *After Virtue*, 216; Schank, *Tell Me a Story*, 170; and Newbigin, *The Gospel in a Pluralistic Society*, 15.

29. Ricoeur, *Time and Narrative*, 246–48.

30. Kidd, *Culture and Identity*, 107.

31. Steffen, *Foundational Roles of Symbol and Narrative*, 477–94.

32. Lamb, *The Art and Craft of Storytelling*, 5.

33. Wiggins and McTighe, *Understanding by Design*. See also Egan, *Teaching as Story Telling*, 25–26.

characters, plot, storyline, ideal/un-ideal archetypes, and foils, story creates a comprehensive whole.[34] It is this characteristic that is the true power of story, that is, "the comprehensive whole." If a storyteller extracts isolated stories from the whole biblical story, the very power of story itself is extricated also.

Story Simplifies a Cosmology

A reflective story can make sense of chaos by providing a plot for the hearer.[35] Story organizes events,[36] identifies archetypes, both ideal and un-ideal,[37] alerts us to obstacles, and reveals the heroines and heroes whom we emulate and the rogues we should avoid.

Within a community the common story is a cosmological script. "A script is a set of expectations about what will happen next".[38] Based on the script, one knows how to act and is able to predict how others will react. Story makes clear what ought and ought not to happen. The common story provides common sense. In other words, story script is the basis for values. Interrelated scripts make up a whole story-based structure or worldview.

Story Speaks Metaphorically

Stories contain images that are imbued with meaning.[39] That imagery is transferred when the story is told, not just in the oral language, but also in all its associated nonverbal paralinguistic elements[40].[41] "Metaphors lodge truth in the imagination".[42] Story and meaning are inextricably linked.

Jerome Bruner argues that story is the praxis of social interaction.[43] Bradt illustrates, "When bushes burst into flame, [Moses] did not think to

34. Ryken, *Words of Delight*, 53–89.

35. Simmons, *The Story Factor*, 37.

36. MacDonald, *The Story-Teller's Start-Up Book*, 31.

37. Ryken, *Words of Delight*, 25–29.

38. Schank, *Tell Me a Story*, 7.

39. Ryken, *Words of Delight*, 13.

40. Nonverbal communication includes symbol elements such as: gestures, physical appearance, physical environment, touch, facial expressions, voice quality, eye contact, proximity, and chronemics.

41. Lipman, *Improving Your Storytelling*, 19, 41–74.

42. Sweet, *Post-Modern Pilgrims*, 89.

43. Bruner, J., *Acts of Meaning*, 77.

measure the angles of the branches or the intensity of the flame's heat but removed his shoes, listened, heard, and knew that he was on holy ground. When seas parted, [Miriam] did not calculate the pull of the planets on the tides; she broke into song and danced her way across starfish and seashell to the safety of dry land and deliverance".[44]

Not only is story a metaphor for life,[45] it is a metaphor of meaning. Wright says, "Stories . . . are the crucial agents that invest events with meaning. The way the bare physical facts are described, the point at which tension or climax occurs, the selection and arrangement—all these indicate the meaning which the event is believed to possess".[46]

Stories Combine to Create a Larger Narrative

Jim Harrison writes, "The answer is always in the entire story, not a piece of it".[47] The optimal insight into the narrative world is to understand the role of narrative in creating the overarching metanarrative.[48] In the presentation of the Bible, we must move beyond simply converting the doctrinal topics from systematic textbooks into small bits delivered in story formats. Simply changing the form of content delivery is not the secret to effective communication.

Furthermore, the whole of the biblical narrative is more significant than picking the top ten stories from the Old and New Testaments. If one only converts topics to a story format or simply chooses the top stories in the Bible, these well-intended remedies actually fall short. Is it possible that these approaches may simply be continuations of the same methodologies that historically have caused Christo-paganism (see Peter Block, 1993, p. 208, regarding culture change)? Neither addresses an overarching worldview.

It is the whole biblical canon as a source of authority and truth in contemporary culture that is important to the cross-cultural worker. "Without paying attention to what has gone before, the great final act may be thrilling but incomprehensible. We are actors in a great drama, but we don't know how to play our roles unless we study the earlier acts the Playwright has written".[49]

44. Bradt, *Story as a Way of Knowing*, xiii.

45. McKee, *Story*, 25.

46. Wright, *The New Testament and the People of God*, 79.

47. Harrison, *a quote attributed to Harrison* in Simmons, *The Story Factor*.

48. Wright, *The New Testament and the People of God*, 37–80.

49. Neff, "Remember the Sea," 68.

Describing current strategies and methodologies of storytelling Michael Goheen writes, "We have fragmented the Bible into bits—moral bits, systematic-theology bits, devotional bits, historical-critical bits, narrative bits. When the Bible is broken up in this way there is no comprehensive grand narrative to withstand the power of the comprehensive humanist narrative that shapes our culture".[50]

Note carefully Goheen's insight regarding narrative bits. The objective of storytelling is not merely an adjustment in the delivery of curriculum content where hard facts are converted to story. Narrative must involve a patient and careful building of a comprehensive framework that is new, mysterious, and holistic—a worldview framework rooted in the Bible itself. In fact, the whole of the Bible is the comprehensive framework—the overarching meta-narrative. Leland Ryken argues, "the whole story is the meaning".[51]

Yes, hypotheses, assumptions, and presuppositions are embedded in story, but when they are removed from the story context—the teller, hearer, story world, and story line—the overarching framework of God's view of reality is diminished. A proposition that has been dedramatized[52] has little to no communicative function.[53] In an attempt to promote story versus propositional truth, some writers have presented story and proposition in a juxtaposition of tension. Such need not be the case, particularly when it comes to a narrative approach to communication.

Story is not in opposition to propositional truth, but rather story illuminates propositional truth.[54] The question should not be, "Which is superior?" Rather, the question is about sequence. Which precedes which?

Mark Johnson, a Professor at the University of Oregon, takes us beyond symbols and embedded propositions to schemata that exist in a continuous, analog fashion.[55] He defines schema as "a recurrent pattern, shape, and regularity".[56] Ordered schemata emerge as meaningful structures by which we comprehend and organize what we encounter.[57]

---

50. Goheen, *The Power of the Gospel*, 5–6.

51. Ryken, *Words of Delight*, 19, 88.

52. Vanhoozer, *The Drama of Doctrine*, 91.

53. Callow, *Man and Message*, 155.

54. Miller, *Story and Context*, 132.

55. Johnson, *The Body in the Mind*, 23.

56. Ibid., 29.

57. For an in-depth analysis of schemata from the perspective of biological

Bradt argues that human knowing, thinking, and consciousness are inextricably tied to a mode of communication, namely story. He writes, "Story is not just an art form or literary genre but a way of structuring thought.[58] Ken Gnanakan's call to "recover the significance" of the creeds[59] will be only answered by "reclaiming story".[60] Note below how Bradt describes the interworking of the component parts in alignment to the whole:

> Knowledge that comes in and through the action of storing is mediated as a holographic whole: that is, it is formed by the dynamic interacting of parts together and reveals itself from multiple perspectives and dimensions through multiple modalities simultaneously. Any attempts to isolate, analyze, or separate out any of the individual operations of this contemporaneous contextual event of knowing would destroy the singleness and unity of the experience; it is by its very nature and constitution, intrinsically multimodal and must be grasped as such.[61]

The parts of the biblical story cannot be isolated or separated from the contemporaneous context of the metanarrative if the hearer is to fully understand the meaning of the component parts. Ryken writes, "We must . . . describe and interpret the details accurately, but it is finally the whole story that embodies the theme".[62] In other words, it is imperative that we see the whole of Scripture as a complete system where the whole is greater than the sum of the parts.[63] In systems thinking the parts cannot be understood in isolation from the whole. Rather than fragmentation, in the whole, the parts are interrelated and interdependent.

Furthermore, the story hearer is drawn into the story. Bradt continues that storying demands interactive relationships of personal presence in the here-and-now.[64] The bits of systematic theology[65] can be "unmoored

---

anthropology, see *The Symbolic Species: The Co-Evolution of Language and the Brain* (1997) by Terrence W. Deacon.

58. Bradt, *Story as a Way of Knowing*, 233.

59. Gnanakan, *Responsible Stewardship*, 24.

60. Bradt, *Story as a Way of Knowing*, 88.

61. Ibid., 12.

62. Ryken, *Words of Delight*, 82.

63. The whole is greater than the sum of the parts. Water illustrates. Water (H2o) as a whole has the characteristic of wetness. Neither of the separated component parts does.

64. Bradt, *Story as a Way of Knowing*, 233.

65. Goheen, *The Power of the Gospel*.

from interests" and disconnected from overarching, pertinent, and real questions.[66] If all the hearer hears is narrative bits, the hearer will not interpret narrative bits through the comprehensive whole of the Bible, but through the existing metanarrative in which he already sees himself. He already is "in a story," whether Mahayana Buddhism, Folk Islam, or secular materialism.[67]

Richard Bauckham, Anglican scholar, writes that a metanarrative:

> . . . is an attempt to grasp the meaning and destiny of human history as a whole by telling a single story about it; to encompass, as it were, all the immense diversity of human stories in a single, overall story which integrates them into a single meaning . . . a single story about the whole of human history in order to attribute a single integrated meaning to the whole. It is a totalizing

---

66. Wiggins and McTighe, *Understanding by Design*, 138.

67. Written as a polemic to the cultures of the Ancient Near East (ANE), cultural cosmologies that were polytheistic, animistic, and holistic at their core (Frankfort, *Ancient Egyptian Religion*), the narrative of Genesis in the Bible begins with God's description of real time/space history. Genesis starts the rival story to the ANE cosmologies, thus setting the stage for worldview transformation. Genesis 1:1 serves as the introduction not only to the first eleven chapters of the book of Genesis or the Pentateuch, but also to the whole Bible.

Rather than a linear argument through perhaps a syllogism, God begins the dramatic narrative of Scripture with the story of creation. The interconnected storyline continues throughout the Bible, building the framework of God's view of reality and, as such, the ultimate foundation for all meaning. God Himself is the protagonist of the story. In every way and in every place, the Bible is theocentric. God defines origin, purpose, destiny, morality, structures, who is man, what is non-man, boundaries (does a man turn into a tiger and a tiger into a man?), relationships (born out the Triune God Himself), cause and effect, power, and hierarchy.

In the first eleven chapters of Genesis alone, the hearer "sees" the reality of one Sovereign God who is moral and predictable. The gods of the Ancient Near East cosmologies were neither. The storyline introduces: values (God saw that the light was good), designations (he separated light from darkness; "A" is "A" and "A" is not "non-A"), time, space (God called the expanse "sky"), history set in motion (there was evening and there was morning—the second day), ecological systems, God's sovereign control over all His creation, the uniqueness of mankind (created in the image of God), human responsibility in the creation, God's goodness and kindness (the Provider of food, heat, rest, and enjoyment), God as the source of life, the introduction of epistemology, theodicy, the origin of sin, the cause of death, delegation, the institution of marriage, the ability to be self-aware, procreation, accountability for sin, a line of people who are God-fearers, man's helplessness in his sin, judgment, covenant relationships, God's faithfulness in remembering mankind, both God's transcendence and immanence, human government, and much more. All this is embedded in the Genesis 1–11 story! The context is real time/space history.

framework, one which tries to subsume everything within its concept of the truth.[68]

The overarching story validates or invalidates all other stories.[69] Note Donald Carson application of this critical truth to the use of Scripture.

> The Bible as a whole document tells a story, and, properly used, that story can serve as a meta-narrative that shapes our grasp of the entire Christian faith. In my view it is increasingly important to spell this out to Christians and to non-Christians, as part of our proclamation of the gospel. The ignorance of basic Scripture is so disturbing in our day that Christian preaching that does not seek to remedy the lack is simply irresponsible.[70]

Hiebert and colleagues argue that "ultimately, meaning is to be found in the cosmic story: the 'big' story about the beginning, meaning, and ending of all things".[71] "The good news story of the Bible should be told as a whole".[72]

Story Can Be Divided into Component Parts

In Western culture we expect to see at least three basic components in a well-told story. They include: (a) setting (time and place), (b) characters, and (c) plot or storyline. The setting is the time and location of the story. The characters in a story must be vivid and believable. The key to a good story is the development of its main characters. The plot or storyline contains the theme or purpose of the story, a movement of action—the organization and sequence of events, perhaps a dramatic dialogue, and the resolution. If story describes the overall journey, "plot is the road it takes to get there".[73] Story is what you know at the end; plot is what you see along the way.

The component parts of story may differ across cultures. Book four in the series, "There is More to the Story", addresses the critical cultural competence of storytelling across cultures. John Cosby describes localized storytelling.

68. Bauckham, *Bible and Missions*, 86–87.

69. Ward, *Teach Yourself Postmodernism*.

70. Carson, *The Gagging of God*, 84.

71. Hiebert et al., *Understanding Folk Religion*, 115.

72. Ibid., 278.

73. Dunne, *Emotional Structure*, 11.

Story Provides a Universal Medium

The story format is not simply for children, a common, but false assumption in Western societies. Story is a global phenomenon, used by all human beings. Seymour writes, "Stories mark us as human".[74] Walter Fisher, in *Human Communication as Narrative*, argues that the *root metaphor* for humanity is "Homo narrans".[75] Stories are intrinsic to humanity and a universal form of communication.

From the popular movie *Australia* starring Nicole Kidman to the mother in the barrio of Córdoba, Argentina who was explaining to her six-year-old boy who I was, to the evangelical pastor in Jogjakarta, Indonesia who was recounting how widespread the Selamatan ceremonies are on the Island of Java, storytelling is the communication mode of choice.

Looking through the grid of intercultural communication, most people in the world are high context and holistic. In other words, meaning in communication is derived from the surrounding environment, the setting, the relationship between sender and receiver, and all the facets of nonverbal cues. Story format provides the natural medium for meaning transfer.

Although a universal medium, storytelling may not always have a universal format. People across cultures tells stories in different ways. The book series addresses this phenomenon and provides an analytical template to determine how to storytell across cultures.

WHAT THE BIBLE INCLUDES

Rather than merely a book of theology, the Bible is a unique work of literature with stories, poems, and letters. Insistently, it is not an outline of theology with accompanying proof texts.[76] No pages are devoted to pneumatology or supralapsarianism. As such, it is not a work of systematic theology. Theological doctrines are most often embedded within the stories. Students of Scripture know that not every part of the Bible is narrative. There is also exposition.

Essentially, there are three types of writing in the Bible. As an adaptation of Ryken, Table 5.1 analyzes, illustrates, and explains the purpose of each biblical type.

74. Seymour, *Creating Stories that Connect*, 9.

75. Fisher, *Human Communication as Narrative*, 62.

76. Ryken, *Words of Delight*, 11.

	Historical	Literature	Exposition
Reference	1 Kings 16:29	Genesis 3:1	Ephesians 2:4
Illustration	"In the thirty-eighth year of Asa king of Judah, Ahab the son of Omri began to reign over Israel . . ." (ESV)	"Now the serpent was more subtle than any other wild creature the LORD God had made. He said to the woman, "Did God say . . ." (NIV)	"But God, being rich in mercy, because of the great love with which he loved us . . ." (ESV)
Explanation	Conveys factual data about the characters and events, all within a moral framework	Recreates concrete experiences and vivid human sensations	Clarifies abstract concepts
Means	Realistic narration	Storytelling	Didactic teaching
Literary device	Data grounded in space/time history	Symbol and metaphor; master images (archetypes)	Precepts of theology
Meaning conveyance	Through literary realism	Through form—settings, characters, and events	Through interpretation
Experiential learning	What happened descriptively	Why it happened	What it asserts normatively
Response	The details tell me the story is credible.	My experiences are exactly the same!	I understand; now I see what it means.
Composition	Three-fourths of the Bible		One-fourth
Conclusion	An anthology of expositional storytelling		

Table 5.1: Analysis of Ryken's Three Types of Writing in the Bible[77]

77. Literary portions of the Bible are often clarified by what is contained in the expository parts (Ryken, *Words of Delight*, 29).

As one analyzes the Bible as a whole, it is an anthology of expositional storytelling. The stories are not simply told. They are exposited. The great Storyteller does not assume that the meaning is clear. It is made clear.

WHAT EXPOSITION ADDS[78]

Anyone familiar with the orality movement as it has evolved in the history of Christian expansion knows the negativity attributed to activity practitioners within the movement call *exposition*. We argue here that the negativity associated with this term is derived from the following assumptions, some false and others true. Some of these assumptions were addressed in Chapter 2.

1. Story, if told well, is self-explanatory.

2. Stories from the Bible are particularly powerful . . . presumably even more self-explanatory than a so-called secular story.[79]

3. The Holy Spirit is the unobserved augmenting power that is able to make the meaning clear.

4. Some hearers understand better by way of story format.

5. Effective storytelling does not need exposition.

6. Topical preaching is confused with narrative exposition.[80]

7. Some expository preachers have acquired a reputation of being boring and ineffective.

8. Narrative exposition is not used skillfully.

---

78. The term *exposition* means "the activity of explaining to make the meaning and purpose clear". Its Latin etymology relates to the concept of exposure. In the Orality Movement, this term is viewed somewhat negatively and its activity is minimized or even excluded. "Each story should be kept free from expositional content" (from *A Methodology for Presenting the Gospel to Oral Communicators*, 2001, IV.4). Going further, Simon Perry writes, "Jesus didn't do expository preaching! Neither did anyone else in the New Testament. Neither should we" (retrieved from http://simonperry.org.uk/exposition/4550415875).

79. "Then Philip ran up to the chariot and heard the man reading Isaiah the prophet. "Do you understand what you are reading?" Philip asked. 'How can I,' he (Ethiopian eunuch) said, 'unless someone explains it to me?' So he invited Philip to come up and sit with him" (Acts 8:30–31, NIV). Note that Scripture refutes its own self-explanatory nature.

80. Robinson, *Biblical Preaching*, 56.

9. Skillful narrative exposition[81] is difficult, therefore avoided, despite the fact that the screenwriting industry and beyond agree it is a necessary mode of rhetorical discourse along with narration, description, and argumentation.

10. Further explanation is needed.

Exposition: A Function within Story Versus a Rival of Story

In a book about strategic storytelling, here is a section devoted to exposition. Is not this an oxymoron, combining two normally contradictory terms? No. Storytellers, whether orators or writers, know that narrative exposition is an indispensable part of skillful storytelling. Rather than accepting exposition as an approach that is at tension with storytelling, we suggest that exposition is a function in the overall process of communicating through story. It is not a method like storytelling. Storytelling is a format in which relevant information is arranged. Within the story, exposition functions to merge animation with definition.[82]

Gabriel Fackre, an American theologian and ecumenist, has written about storytelling for twenty-five years. Note his explanation of the way exposition makes meaning of what the narrator animates.

> The recovery of imagination in the work of theology must not be juxtaposed to rational inquiry and conceptual formulation. Story, metaphor, and visual symbol make their appearance alongside discursive exposition. Wilbur Urban, anticipating many of these modern developments in *Language and Reality*, argues for the complement of "symbolic truth" and the "truth of the symbol." The power of symbol and saga enables us to make our engagement (symbolic truth), and the latter is the conceptual assertion of the fact, not the fiction, of the One who comes (the truth of the symbol).[83]

81. Skillful narrative exposition includes plausible placement of explanatory detail whereby it feels natural to the hearer/reader. It should be dispersed here and there as an organic part of the story. Often exposition can be hidden in dramatic action (watch *Schindler's List* written by Stephen Zaillian—30 minutes into the film).

82. Cassirer, *The Philosophy of Symbolic Forms*, 288.

83. Fackre, *Christ's Ministry and Ours*, 6.

Furthermore, the backstory supplied through exposition gives a kind of information seldom attained in real life, even among personal friends.[84] Consider the ancient story of Job where the unnamed author writes, "There was a man in the land of Uz, whose name was Job; and that man was perfect and upright, one that feared God, and eschewed evil." Here is insight from the divine narrator, who presumes to pass judgment, closed to humans, on Job's spiritual life.

As an expert on rhetorical discourse, Ryken offers these inimitable insights:

> The primary literary rule of interpretation is meaning through form. Whatever a story communicates, it communicates through setting, character, and action. It is therefore necessary, not frivolous, to interact with a biblical story as a story. But if this is a necessary part of understanding biblical narrative, it is not sufficient in itself. It is true that stories convey part of their truth simply by getting us to share an experience with the characters in the story. But any complete understanding of a story depends on our ability to formulate the intellectual truth of the story as well—not as a substitute for the imaged reality of the settings, characters, and events, but as an interpretive lens through which we see their significance. All of this is a way of saying that we need a methodology for getting from the story to the theme—from setting, character, and plot to an intellectual grasp of what the story is about and the perspective that the writer expects us to take toward that subject.[85]

If Ryken is correct, then the implications are enormous and the ramifications, colossal. Storytelling without exposition belies the very intent of the Scriptures themselves. All screenwriters know the necessity of skilled narrative exposition. These assertions are consistent with models of learning created by David Kolb[86] and L. Dee Fink[87]. Both social scientists argue that effective learning goes beyond concrete experience and reflective observation (story). It includes abstract conceptualization where the learner moves from the sphere of apprehension to comprehension.[88]

---

84. Booth, *The Rhetoric of Fiction*, 3.

85. Ryken, *Words of Delight*, 81.

86. Kolb, *Experiential Learning*.

87. Fink, *Creating Significant Learning Experiences*.

88. Wayne Booth, George Pullman Distinguished Service Professor Emeritus at the University of Chicago, provides a clear explanation of how narrators are able to move hearers and readers toward intended meaning in *The Rhetoric of Fiction, Second Edition*

Exposition: An Intention within Story versus a Rival to Story

Rather than a method, exposition is not only a function but also an intention. As such, exposition is not in conflict with storytelling. The storyteller uses narrative skillfully by laying foundation for meaning and artfully, intermittently supplying the backstory to fill in blanks.

The intent of communication is multi-purposed:

1. To develop relationships

2. To create harmony and/or dissonance

3. To transmit emotion

4. To effectively exchange meaning (create understanding)[89]

5. To clearly inform and compellingly influence

J.O. Terry from the Southern Baptists suggests, "There are many peoples . . . historically resistant to traditional Christian witness" because they see teaching as imperialistic (Terry, "In Defense of Storying"). In response, the authors suggest that imperialism, which dehumanized populations throughout the colonized world, is the problem, not the mode of delivery. The appropriate discussion is not to establish a false dichotomy between teaching and storying, but to judge paternalism for what it is.[90]

(1983). See Chapter Seven—The Uses of Reliable Commentary (169–210). "Most of the great storytellers of all periods have found it useful to employ direct judgment, whether in the form of descriptive adjectives or extended commentary" (183). Kathleen Callow stresses the importance of making the relational framework explicit in cross-cultural settings (Callow, *Man and Message*, 329).

89. In an overemphasis on particularism (storying the birth of Jesus to the oppressed), Boomershine errantly states, "What Luke's narrative will mean I cannot predict or foretell" (Boomershine, *Story Journey*, 38). We argue two salient points. First, the narrative of Luke does have primary and secondary meaning embedded in the text itself [Note the assumption of Luke himself, the author, "Having carefully investigated everything from the beginning, I also have decided to write a careful account . . . so you can be certain of the truth" (Luke 1:3–4, New Living Translation)]. Several have reacted strongly to Boomershine's characterization of the biblical story as "a broad playground of meaning" with listeners "invited to play" (Ibid., 52). Acts 4:12 more accurately communicates the exclusivity and eternality. Secondly, the cross-cultural worker must be able to predict the responses of the hearer based upon an understanding of local culture and language. This is basic to any communicative interaction. The implications for the cross-cultural worker are that he has been resident in the host society, has built genuine friendships, has acquired culture and language to an established skill level, and understands the basic core worldview assumptions in the locale.

90. The paternal imperialists, whether representatives of King Leopold of Belgium

This false dichotomy is hindering the best practice of storytelling. Exposition and storytelling are not juxtaposed. In actuality they work hand in glove. A thesis of the book is that exposition and storytelling are inextricable in effective intercultural communication in the global context. We tell to teach. If stories are told apart from exposition, which they are in some quarters, misunderstanding is inevitable.

A sender encodes the message of story through a cultural worldview grid. But the receiver from a culturally different local context decodes the message of story through an altogether different cultural worldview grid. Just because a message is delivered in the medium of oral or written story does not resolve the basic issue in communication of encoding and decoding.[91] On the other hand, if a didactic message is delivered devoid of a story format, that is, through an outline or PowerPoint bullets, communication is greatly diminished.

Of particular apprehension to the authors is the suggestion that a story should be told without interruption in a cross-cultural setting. Some storytellers hastily assume that uninterrupted storytelling is normative among

---

in the Congo (renamed Zaire by Joseph-Desire Mobutu, but now the Democratic Republic of Congo) or British administrators in the Sudan who forbade travel between the Arab north and African south, did their damage on the continent of Africa because of their core worldview assumptions related to people. Cultural evolution drove Northern Europe to "civilize" the savages (note the writings of Lewis Henry Morgan and Edward Tyler). African scholars write that today "the cultural foundations of virtually all African nations remain undefined," a "post-colonial trauma" with a "mish-mash of traditional, colonial, and neo-colonial identities" (Lassiter, "African Culture and Personality" in *African Studies Quarterly*). Nowhere on the continent is this trauma more apparent than in the Sudan. The Comprehensive Peace Agreement signed in January 2005 between the Government of Sudan and the Sudan People Liberation Movement is fragile indeed. Few anticipated a peaceful referendum in January 2011. Why? These woes are the inevitable outcomes of decades of subjugation by ruthless rulers.

In contrast, when George Walker and Bob Kennel presented the Gospel to the Bisorio people in Papua New Guinea, they story-taught the whole biblical story from Genesis forward. Previously, they had established authentic friendships with the Bisorio people. They lived in a village just off a tributary of the Sepik River. They studied Bisorio culture and were competent in the language. Fighting the past momentum and propensity of paternalism, they first gave their lives to the Bisorio people in service and friendship. From a context of love and acceptance, they story-taught the Bible. Their expositional storytelling was not viewed as an imperialistic imposition. If a cross-cultural worker hears from an audience of people the accusation of imperialism, one should first investigate paternalism rather than a method of delivery.

91. For further consideration, see Paul Ricoeur's essay entitled "Explanation and Understanding" (71–88) in *Interpretation Theory: Discourse and the Surplus of Meaning* (1976, Texas Christian University Press).

pre-literate people. Such is not often the case. Here and there are anecdotal accounts in support of the uninterrupted approach, but missiologists must ask themselves about the *validity* and *reliability* of these informal accounts. The authors use these two terms as they are represented in the discipline of qualitative research design.[92]

Some examples suggest interrupted storytelling is, in some cultures, actually the more common method. The Mahabharata, written in Sanskrit and dating to the eight-century BCE, is the longest epic poem in the world. Full of devotional and philosophical material, the entire epic is purportedly told by a bard to a family chief. In the first book (one of eighteen) of the epic, the listener asks the teller questions throughout and the tale develops in response. In the case of the Mahabharata, story is developed through dialogue, not uninterrupted monologue.

Judith Martin of Arizona State University and Tom Nakayama are intercultural scholars who specialize in communication across cultures. Both are Fellows in the International Academy of Intercultural Research (IAIR). They write, "When we negotiate meaning, we are creating, maintaining, repairing, or transforming reality. This implies that people are actively involved in the communication process. One person cannot communicate alone".[93] To argue that storytelling is an uninterrupted attempt at communication belies the very essence of communication itself.

"A good teacher is not one who explains things correctly but one who couches explanations in a memorable format".[94] More directly, good teaching uses storytelling. Storytelling is teaching. The experiential nature of story makes for best teaching. Consider the cliché, "Experience is the best teacher." In her book *Whoever Tells the Best Stories WINS*, Annette Simmons devotes an entire chapter to teaching stories.[95] Similarly, Kevin Vanhoozer states that mere repetition of a story does not necessarily advance our understanding of what the story means.[96]

---

92. For a thorough presentation of storytelling across cultures, see *The World of Storytelling* (1991) by Anne Pellowski.

93. Martin and Nakayama, *Intercultural Communication*, 94.

94. Schank, *Tell Me a Story*, 15.

95. Simmons, *Whoever Tells the Best Stories*, 79–97.

96. Vanhoozer, *The Drama of Doctrine*, 95.

STRATEGIC STORYTELLING

Ryken argues, "Truth is more than propositional, and the Bible implicitly acknowledges this by giving us truth partly in a literary medium".[97] Through the genre of literature, truth is embedded in life, human experience, and reality. As a work of literature, Scripture recreates the actual scenes in sufficient detail to allow the reader/hearer to imaginatively experience them. Through the medium of story, the precepts are brought to life. The story format itself embodies the meaning. One's worldview is far more than intellect and idea. We understand who we are, what we are to do, and what is real through images, metaphors, and stories.[98] The medium by which truth is conveyed itself is the message.

Story is like a lion, the king of the jungle. Presenting precepts through bulleted PowerPoint presentations is like tranquilizing the lion to clip off tufts of hair from its mane. One can present tufts to an audience, but likely the presenter will need to show the image of the lion to identify the real meaning of the clustered strands of hair. One of the most often repeated refrains during a PPT presentation is, "Let me illustrate this by telling a story . . . " Reformatting precepts into short narrative bits is like cutting off the lion's front paw for presentation purposes—a deadly approach. A better way is not to stop the lion, but let it roam.

American historian Lewis Mumford helps us understand the power of metaphor by noticing the role and function of a clock. Prior to the fourteenth-century, men looked toward the sun and the seasons. The clock has made us look at seconds and minutes. So poignant is this reality, Mumford argues, that the ticking of the clock weakened the supremacy of God, where in the past Eternity served as the measure and focus of human events.[99]

Concerning the power of medium and metaphor, Neil Postman describes how the alphabet introduced a new form of conversation between man and man. Now one can *see* an utterance rather than only hear it. The advent of writing *froze* speech and gave birth to the grammarian, the

---

97. Ryken, *Words of Delight*, 15.

98. Niebuhr, *A Nation So Conceived*, 161.

99. Mumford, *Technics and Civilization*.

rhetorician, the historian, and the scientist.[100] Metaphors, as collapsed stories, create the content of our culture.[101][102]

CONCLUDING REFLECTIONS

What story did we tell about what story is and what it does? We shared that story recounts lived experiences and if skillfully told it will draw the hearer into the story. In the chapter that follows, we will unpack the details of a solution. Rather than quickly rushing toward a solution, our purpose has been to model the methodology by laying foundation.

Based upon these foundational chapters, what follows is a full staging of what to do and how to do it.

100. Postman, *Amusing Ourselves to Death*, 12.

101. Ibid., 15.

102. For a scholarly look at the function of written texts, consider *Is There a Meaning in this Text? The Bible, the Reader, and the Morality of Literary Knowledge* (1998) by Kevin J. Vanhoozer.

6

Examining a Solution

Steps 1–5

INTRODUCTORY REMARKS

GIVEN THE IMPERATIVE TO carry out ministry in the cross-cultural setting at a worldview level, we propose a methodology of *strategic storytelling*. The methodology assumes two things: (a) that analyzing culture is a path toward understanding worldview and (b) that storytelling leads to effective communication across cultures.

There is a chronology to the method. It takes time and unfolds over time. It has starting and ending points. There is a procedure to the method. It includes twelve steps carried out systematically. There are underlying philosophies to the method (see Chapter 9). We begin with the first five steps of the twelve-step process described with detail in the vernacular of story.

STEP 1: INVESTIGATE THE STORYLANDS

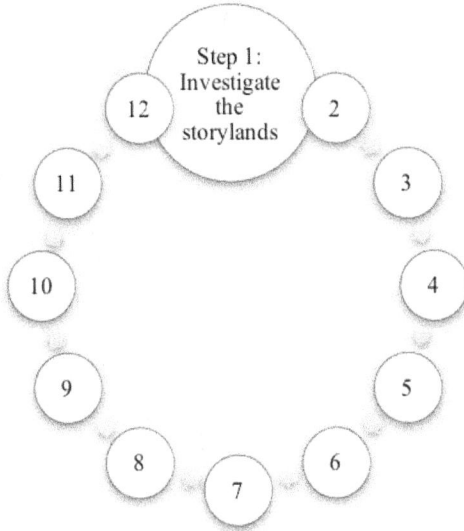

Figure 6:1: Investigate

The first step (see Figure 6:1) in *strategic storytelling* calls for the investigation of the storylands by reviewing current and precedent academic literature.[1] Other data collection techniques are also useful, such as observation (direct and participant) and interviews (unstructured at the beginning and structured later). Usually, observation precedes interviewing. Observation provides firsthand experience as well as a general overview. From there, interviews fill in the blanks with increased specificity. Research can commonly be done prior to entering the host society.

Why do research before entering the story? Researching a people group in their historical and geographical context is a primary way to show honor and respect to others. It also prepares one as much as possible for inevitable cultural differences. Thereby, it reduces the stress of cultural adjustment that always accompanies deprivation of norm. It enables the cross-cultural worker to enter the story with a foundation for predicting

---

1. At Purdue University's Online Writing Lab (OWL), insights are available for conducting research in books, academic journals, and online databases. See https://owl. english.purdue.edu/owl/section/2/8/ It is important that the cross-cultural worker understand established techniques for conducting a literature review.

and explaining local structure and events. It demonstrates intercultural sensitivity[2] and cultural intelligence[3].

Strategic storytelling recognizes the need to investigate the storylands first as the cross-cultural worker prepares. What are the three storylands? What follows is an expansion of Step 1.

Storyland of the Bible

The first storyland is the culture of the biblical story. Scripture is made clear by understanding the Ancient Near East. The story of the Bible is set in historical and geographical contexts, namely Mesopotamia, Egypt, and Syria-Palestine. From the Old Testament to the New Testament, the story includes cities, civilizations, cultures, hegemonies, languages, worldviews, chronology, and symbols. Authors of biblical books lived in time/space history. They wrote in languages representing their own cultural framework. An accurate exegesis of Scripture requires knowledge of the Israelite/Hebraic worldview as well as Jewish and Greco-Roman cultures. This knowledge acquisition does not mystically happen. It takes effort. Skill in interpreting and understanding the Bible is acquired over time and through diligent work.

In Medieval times, the Bible was not available to the common person, who was usually poor and illiterate. Reading, interpreting, and sharing Scripture was the work of religious scholars and educated clergy. They had direct access to Scripture that most others did not.

Then, in the late fourteenth-century, the Wycliffe Bible was translated into English. John Wycliffe was the Morning Star of the Reformation. But in 1408 a synod formally outlawed the circulating and reading of the Wycliffe Bible with a corresponding penalty of excommunication from the church. In fact, in 1415, the Council of Constance condemned Wycliffe, exhumed his body, and burned it. Why?

---

2. Milton Bennett (1993) identifies six stages of sensitivity in the Developmental Model of Intercultural Sensitivity (DMIS). The stages range from denial of cultural differences in extreme ethnocentrism to an integration of cultural differences in sophisticated ethnorelativism. See an adaptation of the DMIS model in the Appendices.

3. The Cultural Intelligence Center in Holt, Michigan has designed and developed an assessment of cultural intelligence (CQ). The research has recognized four capabilities of CQ: Drive, Knowledge, Strategy, and Action. Boldly entering a host society and assuming an authoritative voice as an outsider are at worst extreme ethnocentrism or at best a manifestation of low CQ. See more explanation about CQ in the Appendices.

There has perhaps been no more significant event than the printing of the Bible in common languages to advance the Kingdom of God.[4] At the time of the Reformation, however, religious scholars were mortified by the prospect of a common uninformed and untrained person reading and interpreting the Bible. Beyond the motivation of church tyranny, the clergy assumed that the uneducated would not have the requisite skills. Was this concern valid? Should it be a concern today? Yes, it should be. The cross-cultural worker must be informed and trained in the culture of the Bible storyland.

Storyland of the Teller

The second storyland is the culture of the cross-cultural worker. The starting point for all intercultural communication is first understanding oneself.[5] Ancient philosophers argued that knowing oneself, though difficult, was the foundation of wisdom. John Calvin likewise underlined the absolute necessity of self-knowledge at the beginning of his Institutes, putting it on par with knowledge of God.

Knowing one's own culture is no easy task. Edward T. Hall (1914–2009), American anthropologist and cross-cultural researcher, delivers groundbreaking research in his now well-known and widely read books, *The Silent Language* (1959), *The Hidden Dimension* (1966), and *Beyond Culture* (1976). He writes, "Culture hides more than it reveals, and strangely enough what it hides, it hides most effectively from its own participants".[6] In his autobiography Benjamin Franklin writes, "There are three things extremely hard: steel, diamond, and to know one's self".[7][8]

4. See Jack Goody, *The Interface between the Written and the Oral*, 1987, Cambridge University Press.

5. T.S. Eliot, *Four Quartets*: "We shall not cease from exploration, And the end of all our exploring, Will be to arrive where we started, And know the place for the first time."

6. Hall, *The Silent Language*, 29.

7. Franklin, *Poor Richard's Almanack*, 195.

8. Kenneth Pike's work in linguistics (phon*etic*s and phon*emic*s) has also been applied to culture. The insider has an *emic* view of language and culture. For example, I aspirate my initial "t's" but do not know it. In the word "butter", I do not say a "t" but a "flapped r". However, I think I say a "t". I tacitly know how to speak American English but don't really hear phonetically what I am saying. Therefore, when I say *tiempo* (time) in Spanish, I am unaware that I aspirate the "t" and thereby speak with an accent. In terms of culture, the North American insider likely is unaware he is individualistic. Just like the aspirated "t", the *emic* cultural value-dimension is hidden. When a North American is in the presence of a colleague from China, a person who is collectivistic, the typical

If the cross-cultural worker does not understand his own cultural values and assumptions, there is little way to understand the difference between the cross-cultural worker and the host society. Why is this an issue? Most people assume, naturally enough, that others think like they do. They do not. They do not have the same values. They do not think in the same categories. Their core assumptions are likely as different as night and day. They do not story in the same way. They do not build or maintain relationships in the same way. They do not hear the Bible in the same way. They do not lead in the same way.[9]

Rather than parachuting into a ministry context, the aspiring cross-cultural worker should ask the pilot to turn around and land the plane so that he may embark on a quest of self-discovery. Angela Edwards, Elena Steiner, and I have developed the Cultural Context Awareness assessment instrument. It measures the degree to which a cross-cultural worker is aware of his own cultural context as well as his awareness of other cultural contexts.

Storyland of the Hearer

The third storyland is the culture of the host society. Cross-cultural workers must have prior training, formal or nonformal, in cultural anthropology. (Book three in the series, "There is More to the Story", presents an alternative way to study anthropology. Michael Matthews introduces a "Novel Approach" to cultural acquisition and analysis—through the medium of story.) Communication stands or falls with the worker's intercultural skills.

It is on this point more than any other that *strategic storytelling* differs from the bulk of methods espoused by the orality movement. We reject the false hypothesis that communication across cultures, accurate decoding of the biblical metanarrative, displacement of an existing story, and displacement and transformation of worldview all occur through a fiat act of God, a sovereign and authoritative exploit apart from human affordance and agency. We do not believe this is the norm.

---

response of both is to find the other somewhat strange. The Chinese person is also *emic*.

So, I silently assume I know how to function across cultures, how to say *tiempo*, how to minister, or how to tell a story. We all do. But, in fact, many times we have little idea how we are coming across because of the "outside-of-our-awareness" cultural traits.

9. To illustrate, we assume that Robert Greenleaf's precepts of servant leadership are biblical (Greenleaf, *Servant Leadership*). Not all church and mission leaders do.

So, Step 1 is an ongoing process, beginning before one enters the storyland and continuing throughout one's duration in the storyland. Obviously, research should include consultation with others who have studied and lived in the locality. At some point, the storyteller is prepared to enter the story of the host society.[10]

Step 2: Enter the Story

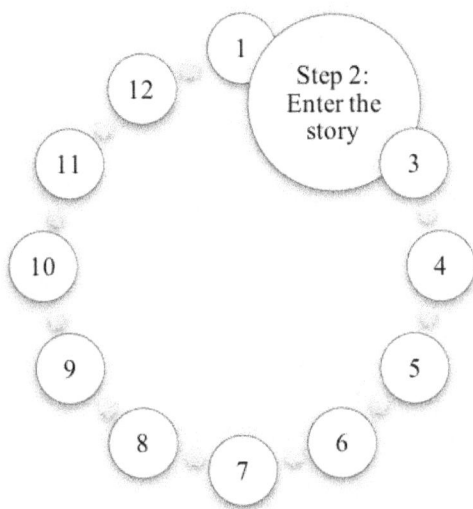

Figure 6.2: Enter the Story

The second step in *strategic storytelling* is to "enter" the story of the host society to establish authentic relationships. There is absolutely no substitute for a "being among the people" approach to cross-cultural ministry. Effectiveness demands immersion. It requires living in the setting among people. Culture and language acquisition are non-optional.

This step pertains to four dynamics: context, connections, credibility, and communication, each of which is enveloped by culture. It is by being

---

10. "It is difficult to conceive that any branch of the human family can be less productive in arrangements, less frugal in enjoyment, less industrious in acquiring, more implacable in their resentments, more ungovernable in their passions, with fewer principles to guide them, with few obligations to restrain them, and with less knowledge to improve and instruct them. We speak of them as they are." This was written by Lewis Cass (1782–1866), Governor of Michigan.

in the cultural context that connections are most effectively made. And it is through connections that trust bonds are developed . . . credibility. And it is by virtue of trust bonds that effective communication across cultures is enabled.[11]

Charles Kraft contributes a unique perspective about communication within cultures. He sees the sender and receiver in communication across cultures in dissimilar contexts with different frames of reference.[12]

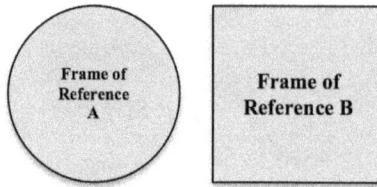

Figure 6.3: Frames of Reference

If person A seeks to communicate with B by speaking entirely in terms of "Frame of Reference A", it is beyond the ability of B to understand A. B is already immersed in "Frame of Reference B". At one time in the history of missions, colonial workers extracted person B from his "Frame of Reference B" to convert B to "Frame of Reference A". This was not salvation but an assumed natural process of cultural evolution. After all, it was assumed A was superior to B. Cultural evolution was based upon the assumption that humans transitioned from savages to barbarians to civilized persons.

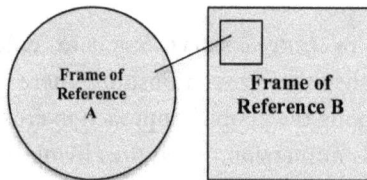

Figure 6.4: Being Among the People

In a "being among the people" approach to cross-cultural ministry, A enters into the context of B. Pre-entry research (Step 1) informs the ideal

11. See the work of Marvin Mayers on "trust bonds" and the "prior question of trust" (Mayers, *Christianity Confronts Culture*).

12. Kraft, *Christianity in Culture*, 154.

geographic location in a host society and the manner of entry. Considerations include: physical acclimation (climate, lodging, diet, and lifestyle procedures), regional permissions/sponsorship for "transfer of trust", respect of local norms, and residency/migration patterns of local populations.

Consistent with *strategic storytelling*, A seeks to communicate with B in the context of B by first establishing a basis for communication within "Frame of Reference B", a basis grounded upon connections and credibility. A enters and learns "Frame of Reference B". Of course, this was not done in colonial times. B was a savage and "Frame of Reference B" was the savagery from which B must be extracted. In a "being among the people" approach, B understands A because A is within the context of B, speaks the language of B, respects "Frame of Reference B", has made connections, developed credibility, and contextualizes communication in terms of the categories of "Frame of Reference B".

Kraft writes,

> The most impactful communication results from person-to-person interaction. It is the rubbing of life again life, not simply the sending and receiving of vocal, gestural, or printed symbols that makes for maximum effectiveness in communication. *Messages are made credible or incredible by the nature of their relationship to the life of the sender.* Prolonged involvement of person with person assures intensive and effective communication of a multiplicity of messages transmitted and received both consciously and unconsciously concerning a multiplicity of topics. Communication is most effective when sender, message, and receiver participate in the same frame of reference.[13] (emphasize added)

Note how Kraft's emphasis in this lengthy quote is different from hasty current methodologies where an outsider momentarily enters a host society and shares sketchy story bits. South African missiologist David Bosch agrees with Kraft, arguing that the Gospel takes shape concretely inside of experiential relationships.[14] Or, as Emil Brunner suggests, communicating Christ to others is never merely a proclamation but always a relationship in which truth is encountered.[15] How is this accomplished? *Strategic storytelling* says a cross-cultural worker must "enter" the story of the host society. And this entrance is not momentary.

13. Kraft, *Christianity in Culture*, 149.

14. Bosch, *Transforming Mission*, 19.

15. Brunner, *Truth as Encounter*.

STEP 3: MODEL THE STORY

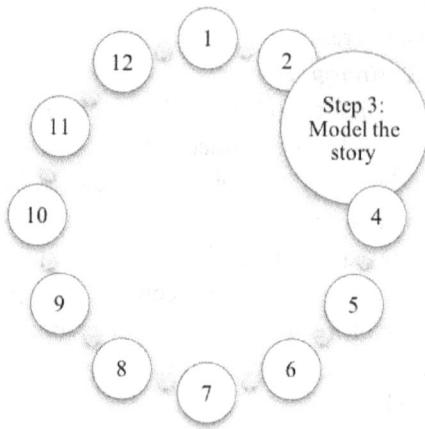

Figure 6.5: Model the Story

Hadith is an Arabic word meaning speech. In common usage it is any tradition passed on orally. Related to Islam and Muhammad, the hadiths represent what the Prophet did, said, or witnessed. Every hadith (and there are 100,000) has two parts: *isnad* (chain of transmission) and *matn* (content). Over time *isnad* has taken precedence over *matn*. If the chain of transmitters is reliable, then so is the content. Reliable people do not relay unreliable content.

Jesus of Nazareth proceeded similarly. As he lived among local people, it was his imperative to establish his authority (Matthew 7:28; 9:7; 21:23f; 28:18; Mark 1:27; John 1:12; 5:27; 10:18; 17:2). Almost his entire public ministry was carried out in region of Galilee, in and out from the city of Capernaum on the north side of the Lake of Gennesaret. "Jesus and his companions went to the town of Capernaum, and every Sabbath day he went into the synagogue and taught the people. They were amazed at his teaching, for he taught as one who had real authority—quite unlike the teachers of religious law" (Mark 1:21–22, NLT). Jesus immersed himself in local culture and did so for strategic purposes related to his mission. For Jesus, the messenger was the message.

In First Thessalonians 2, the Apostle Paul describes his own manner among followers of God in Thessalonica, a chief Hellenistic town in Macedonia. He and his fellow workers befriended locals, treating them with care and admiration. Specific words and phrases from Paul's descriptive narration are emphasized in the footnote below.[16]

It is *isnad* and *matn*. The credibility of the messenger conveys the credibility of the message. Who is the messenger? What is his message? Is he his message? Does he live it? If I am able to relate to him, if I am like him, will I embrace his message as he does? Is his message important . . . impactful? What is the authority behind his message? What is its history? In what ways will his message change my community, my family, and me?

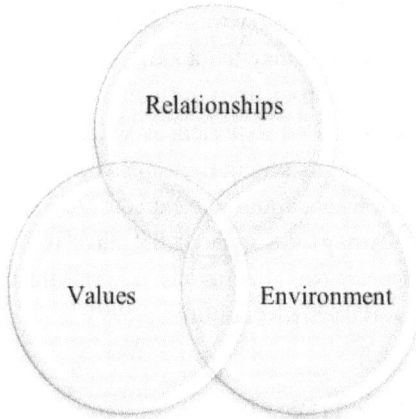

Relationships

Values   Environment

Figure 6.6: Elements of Influence

Leadership theory teaches us that the influence of a leader is determined by three elements: relationships, environment, and values. Studies

16. First Thessalonians 2:4–13 4On the contrary, we speak as those approved by God to be entrusted with the gospel. We are not trying to please people but God, who tests our hearts. 5You know we never used flattery, nor did we put on a mask to cover up greed—God is our witness. 6We were not looking for praise from people, not from you or anyone else, even though as apostles of Christ we could have asserted our authority. 7Instead, *we were like young children* among you. Just *as a nursing mother cares for her children*, 8so *we cared for you*. Because *we loved you so much*, we were delighted to share with you not only the gospel of God but our lives as well. 9Surely you remember, brothers and sisters, our toil and hardship; we worked night and day in order not to be a burden to anyone while we preached the gospel of God to you. 10You are witnesses, and so is God, of how holy, righteous and blameless we were among you who believed. 11For you know that we dealt with each of you *as a father deals with his own children*, 12*encouraging, comforting and urging you* to live lives worthy of God, who calls you into his kingdom and glory. 13And we also thank God continually because, when you received the word of God, which you heard from us, you accepted it not as a human word, but as it actually is, the word of God, which is indeed at work in you who believe. (NIV, Emphasis added)

show that no element is more important than interpersonal relationships developed within a common environment.[17]

Not long ago I was in Guatemala facilitating a seminar about the design and delivery of integral missionary training. The event was hosted in Quetzaltenango by COMIBAM[18], the Ibero-America network of global missions. Afterward, I returned to Guatemala City with a local missionary who described his two-times-a-month Sunday afternoon ministry with indigenous people who lived remotely in the Sierra Madre Mountains. He and his family lived in Guatemala City in a gated and guarded subdivision. How well do you think his ministry was going?

A cross-cultural worker may tell a story from the Bible anywhere in the world. But if it is told apart from authentic relationships with people over time, deprived of shared experiences within a local environment, and without the story hearers seeing the values of the storyteller validated through life situations, what should one expect? Does only the story of the Qur'an need *isnad*? Perhaps the story of the Bible is a wonder story that does not demand display? No. The models in Scripture are clear. We know what we need to be and do across cultures.

STEP 4: COLLECT STORIES

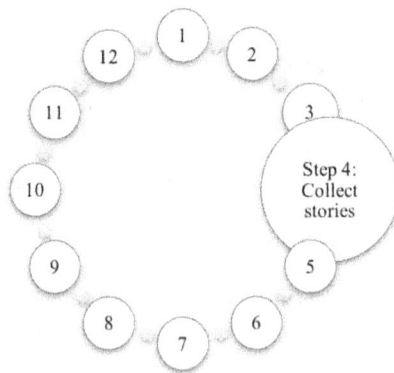

Figure 6.7: Collect Stories

17. Thrall et al., *The Ascent of a Leader*, 44.

18. COMIBAM = Cooperación Misionera Iberoamericana

Ethnography is perhaps the most well-known of the five qualitative approaches[19] to inquiry.[20] "Ethnographers are social scientists who undertake research and writing about groups of people by systematically observing and participating in the lives of the people they study".[21][22] The step-by-step ethnographic process with its methods and techniques is rooted in cultural anthropology.

Raymond Madden sees ethnography as a "storied reality". He writes, "An ethnography is ultimately a story that is backed up by reliable qualitative data and the authority that comes from active ethnographic engagement".[23] The authors of this series agree. What does Madden mean by "ethnographic engagement"? He is referring to Step 2.

Stories are the inimitable resource for defining culture, predicting and explaining behavior, and reframing outcomes. To illustrate the role of discourse in framing a worldview, Bruce Lincoln, professor of the history of religions at the Divinity School of the University of Chicago, describes terrorist activities this way:

> Religious discourse can recode virtually any content as sacred, ranging from the high-minded and progressive to the murderous, oppressive, and banal, for it is not any specific orientation that distinguishes religion, but rather its metadiscursive capacity to frame the way any content will be received and regarded.[24]

Mentioned previously, the book *Master Narratives of Islamist Extremism* (2011) illustrates Madden's view of ethnography as "storied reality". Halverson, Goodall, Jr., and Corman studied the recurring master narratives of Islamists. Their research looked at hundreds of statements by extremists, texts, websites, and online media, produced in multiple languages.

---

19. Other qualitative approaches to inquiry include: narrative, phenomenology, grounded theory, and case study.

20. Creswell, *Qualitative Inquiry.*

21. Madden, *Being Ethnographic*, 1.

22. Extensive and exemplary academic works guide the fieldwork (Agar, 1992; Fetterman, 2010; Goetz and LeCompte, 1984; McCurdy, Spradley, & Shandy, 2004; Pelto & Pelto, 1978; Wolcott, 2008). See the Appendices for a brief list of activities required for social research out in the field.

23. Madden, *Being Ethnographic*, 6.

24. Lincoln, *Holy Terrors*, 6.

A master narrative is "a transhistorical narrative that is deeply embedded in a particular culture".[25] They attain dominance over time through relevance, repetition, and reverence. Master narratives always contain ideal and unideal archetypes—characters, events, and plots that are known to and remembered by all people in a culture. Just the mention of archetypes invokes the whole master narrative without actually telling the story.

Master narratives shape the rhetorical vision in four ways:

1. They enable people in a culture to make sense of everyday life.

2. They connect the present day with the past.

3. People use them to justify current behavior.

4. They tell people what the future will be, and as such, provide a trajectory

To have credibility with people in a culture, master narratives must display six characteristics (see Table 6.1).

Characteristic	Description
Coherent	The narratives must make sense based upon the assumptions of the people group.
Thematic	They must include a collection of systemic stories that elaborate a cultural value.
Real	People must perceive them as comporting with reality.
Meaningful	Each master narrative and any collection of master narratives as a whole make meaning through the way they frame the story.
Prophetic	People will rely on master narratives to reveal trajectory.
Historical	They must be deeply rooted in history, so much so, that they are widely shared, told again and again, and are extremely resistant to change.

Table 6.1: Characteristics of Master Narratives[26]

25. Halverson et al., *Master Narratives*, 14.

26. Compare these empirically based characteristics of master narratives with a hypothetical new ministry setting where a cross-cultural worker, an outsider to the host society, with minimal mastery of local culture and language, shares a rival biblical story with people, but does so hastily, briefly, and in story bits. To what degree will locals sense coherency given their core assumptions about reality? Will story bits be tied together systemically into a whole? Will people perceive the biblical story as real? In what ways will the biblical

What are examples of master narratives from global cultures? The number of master narratives throughout all cultures is incalculable. Here are five that illustrate the characteristics and purposes described above:

1. The story of Pharaoh as told in the Qur'an, Torah, and Pentateuch—The Pharaoh master narrative is told throughout the Arab world to remind people of Allah's faithful redemption of his followers from ruthless oppression. On October 6, 1981, Lieutenant Khalid Islambouli, the leader of the plot to assassinate President Anwar Sadat, leaped from his passing military truck and ran toward the stands where dignitaries were viewing a parade. He with three collaborators lobbed grenades toward the Egyptian President and discharged their automatic weapons. After Islambouli finished firing his assault weapon at Sadat, he cried out, "I have killed the Pharaoh!" Sadat was shot thirty-seven times. Forty people were killed or wounded. Why did the assassin refer to a 3,000-year-old dynasty? This seems strange. In an audio statement released to CNN on November 14, 2002, Osama Bin Laden labeled President George W. Bush, "the Pharaoh of the century". Here was another tie of current events to the Pharaoh. Why? To Muslim hearers, these references are not strange. They are readily understood. The Pharaoh master narrative, deeply rooted in history, gives meaning to current events. To followers of Allah, Sadat and Bush were ruthless oppressors from whom Allah granted deliverance just as he faithfully did millennia ago.

2. September 11, 2001 in Lower Manhattan, New York City, USA

3. The Battle of Karbala—This event is central to the history and tradition of Shia Muslims, one of the minority branches of Islam. It took place on October 10, 680 AD in Karbala, today a holy city in modern Iraq. The Prophet Muhammad's own grandson, Husayn ibn Ali was martyred . . . killed and mutilated by the army of the Umayyad dynasty. Husayn was the third Shia imam, successor of the Prophet. The brief battle was an epic event in Shiite history marking suffering and martyrdom. Today October 10 is a holy day of public mourning and is called Ashura. Husayn represents resistance in the face of oppression. Under the rule of Saddam Hussein, Shia Muslims were greatly

story make meaning, new meaning, that will be understood and emotionally embraced by the people? How will the biblical story reveal a new trajectory? By what means will people in the host society see the biblical narrative as deeply rooted in history? Will the biblical stories be widely shared, told over and over across time, and weather resistance?

restricted from making the expected once-in-a-lifetime pilgrimage to Karbala and non-Iraqi Shia were not permitted to travel there at all.

4. Martin Luther King Jr. and the Civil Rights Movement of the 1960s in the USA—Martin Luther King Jr. (1929–1968) was a Baptist pastor involved in the Civil Rights Movement in the 1950s and 60s in the United States. Born Michael, named after his father, MLK's name was changed to Martin Luther after his father visited Nazi Germany in 1934. Inspired by the nonviolence of Gandhi, MLK promoted nonviolent resistance against the discrimination of black people. On April 4, 1968, while MLK was in Memphis, Tennessee to support a strike by black sanitary public works employees, he was assassinated in the early evening. Despite controversies from plagiarism in his PhD dissertation to allegations of adultery, MLK's legacy remains, remembered for his stand on social justice. Martin Luther King, Jr. Day is observed on the third Monday of January. President Ronald Reagan signed the holiday into law in 1983.

5. The many stories related to the Dirty War (Guerra Sucia) in Argentina and the "disappeared ones"—Starting in the mid-1950s and extending into the early eighties, Argentina like other countries in the Southern Cone of South America were ruled by strongmen and dictators. The government of Argentina with its security forces mercilessly battled leftist guerillas, dissenters, and sympathizers in an effort to hold Marxism at bay. The estimated number of people killed and/or who "disappeared" varies, but ranges from 8,000 to 30,000. Argentines to this day understand the United States Government supported the dictators and atrocities. The goal was to prevent communism from spreading further into Latin America. In his 1964 acceptance speech as the Republican Presidential candidate, Senator Barry Goldwater from Arizona said, "Extremism in the defense of liberty is no vice!" On my first trip to Argentina in 2004, an Argentine colleague asked me what my views were on former Secretary of State Henry Kissinger. Kissinger, born in Germany to German/Jewish parents who immigrated to the USA in 1938, was Secretary of State from 1973 through 1977 in the administrations of Richard Nixon and Gerald Fold. Of course, I was caught off guard. I did not know the history of USG involvement in Latin America and the associated master narratives.

The description of *Step 4: Collect Stories* has been more general than specific. Our first purpose here was to introduce the phenomena of master narratives or what later may be called "anchor stories". What about specifics? How many stories? In qualitative research that is descriptive, Loreen Wolfer suggests 30–250 observations for each hypothesis.[27] How are stories collected across generations, gender, and geographies? At the writing of this book, Elena Steiner at Arizona State University is doing dissertation research on the number of needed master narratives. Her research, related mostly to the United States Department of Defense, will inform the work of cross-cultural Christian workers.

In the book series entitled "There is More to the Story", Mike Matthews introduces a master narrative tool for the ethnographic research described in this book. His book three is entitled *A Novel Approach: The Significance of Story in the Hermeneutic of Reality*. The tool enables a cross-cultural worker to identify the master narratives in a culture and determine how they inform core worldview assumptions and shared value-dimensions with all the resulting socio-cultural institutions and relevant observable behaviors.

STEP 5: ANALYZE STORIES

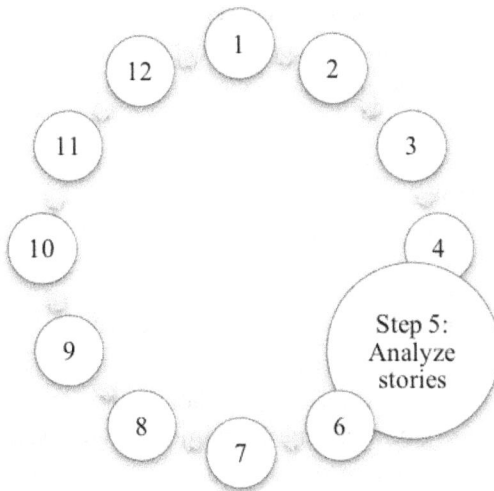

Figure 6.8: Analyze Stories

---

27. Wolfer, *Real Research*, 214–15.

Local, regional, and national master symbols and narratives inform all aspects of culture at every level. These symbols and stories are known to most if not all in the host society. They are the resource by which sense is made. The stories are told and retold at appropriate and relevant events. It is from the controlling stories that one is able to see worldview core assumptions about self, Other, relationships, causality, time, and space. Thereby, self is defined and seen in its relationship with Other.

The repeated story plots reveal cause and effect. Human and nonhuman story characters are engaged on the stage of life in real time and actual space.

Self	Other
Relationships	
Causality	
Time	Space

Table 6.2: Worldview Classifications

The "oughtness" of what should and should not be said and done is evident in the storyline. Across time shared symbols and repeated stories detail the incidents wherein societies formalize and codify value-dimensions, thereby institutionalizing them. Institutionalized norms then require structure and function to maintain the reliability and validity of the shared values. To illustrate this, in civic government, laws created through a legislative process are ordered and enforced by an administrative structure, and finally litigated by a judicial process.

The analytical tools applicable to investigating symbols and stories are similar to those tools used in empirical social research. Through analysis the whole is separated into parts in order to understand the whole. Consider these steps:

1. Successive approximation[28]—Read and reread the collected master narratives. After several readings and much reflection, the observer may be able to see a whole, parts, relationships, causality, categories, order, themes, counterthemes, continuity, and dissonance. At this stage after successive readings (hearings), which themselves are the nearest equivalent to experiencing the culture events for oneself, the culture researcher and analyst only offers approximations. It is too early in the analytical process to form conclusions.

28. Wolfer, *Real Research*, 495.

2. Reflective observation[29]—What are the facts? What is verifiable and what is not? What happened? What should have happened? To whom? By whom? How? When? Where? For what reason(s)? By asking these interrogative questions, the story analyst is able to sort out the characters in the story. The plot and setting are identified and described. Attention is paid to symbols, rituals, story tone, and overall themes and counter-themes. What appears to tie the story together? To connect the characters? What causes the conflict or crisis? What motivates the characters? Again, this early step is not a stage for forming conclusions. Reflective observation is simply answering the question, "What happened?"

3. Abstract conceptualization through a process of coding (open, axial, and selective)—Once the facts of the story seem clear, it is time to answer the question, "So what?" Given that cultural artifacts, images, symbols, rituals, cultural events, and story components have been identified, how do they arrange themselves, relate to each other, and together make meaning?

   a. Open coding—At a surface level of abstraction, "open" coding arranges items into units and units into sub-categories and sub-categories into categories (see Table 6.3 for an example of open coding analysis of symbols). Labels for units, sub-categories, and categories are limitless. Margaret LeCompte and Jean Schensul offer the following: events, activities, behaviors, statements, settings, symbols, factors, variables, models, domains, classes, and categories.[30]

Raw data observed in the field	Open Coding				
+ d 3 a x—4 ! 1 / b c 2 =	First, what are logical categories for the symbols?	3 4 1 2	d a b c	+ x-/ =	!
	Then, what may be a suitable label?	Numbers	Letters	Function Symbol	Punctuation

Table 6.3: An Example of Open Coding Analysis of Symbols

29. Kolb, *Experiential Learning*, 30–31.
30. LeCompte and Schensul, *Analyzing and Interpreting Ethnographic Data*.

b. Axial coding[31]—At a deeper level of abstraction, "axial" coding identifies the relationships among the open codes. What are the connections and intersections? The axis? Axes? It is the causal relationships within or between units that provide the initial foundations for determining meaning. The numbers in the Table 6.3 may be disaggregated and combined with a mathematical function to create an equation like, "$1 + 3 = 4$". The letters "a, b, and d" can form a word, "bad", whose arrangement as a whole has a meaning that the individual component item letters do not have. Enhanced meaning is added with the grammatical punctuation, for example, "bad!" Under what conditions may categories of units be combined? What are the consequences?

c. Selective coding—Finally, "selective" coding is a late phase of analysis that explains causation and abstracts the concepts. It seeks a core category, central themes, and a valid storyline. What is an overall worldview? Finding the core variable(s) means one is able to explain the behavior of culture participants and to understand the structure and function of society. From an *etic* perspective, it is explanation that leads to prediction. Corbin and Strauss provide helpful criteria in Table 6.4 to identify core variables:

	Criteria
	All other categories of data relate to it
	It appears frequently throughout data
A core variable	Variations may be explained; they do not nullify
	Logic and consistency are prevalent
	Additional data only strengthen the conclusion

Table 6.4: Criteria to Determine a Core Variable

4. The analytical process is not done in exclusion. Categories, patterns, and themes are informed by precedent literature. Scholars have already provided theoretical constructs by which the cultural researcher

---

31. Corbin and Strauss, *Basics of Qualitative Research*.

or symbol-story analyst is able make meaning. They provide fundamental frames of reference for inquiry and analysis.[32]

5. Theoretical saturation is a point at which data collection and analysis conclude. It does not mean that all possible data sources have been exhausted, but it does mean that no new data is being found that expands units, sub-categories, and categories.

6. Based upon the results of story analysis, where the cross-cultural researcher has identified the master symbols and narratives that pervade the host society, one is at a point where the big picture story or metanarrative of the culture comes into view.[33] At this point, the cross-cultural worker is ready to begin crafting the biblical story in such a way that it befits the context.

Here is an analytical model for critiquing stories gathered from in the context of the host society:

1. Characters: Who are the protagonists, antagonists, and foils (the supporting characters)? Whose name is repeated? Who has power? Who has authority? Who makes decisions and how are those implemented? Who is able to say what is truth? Who learns from whom and how? Who relates to whom? Who is your favorite character? Least favorite? What are the important groups? How are groups related to each other? What rival stories in the culture will contest stories from the Bible?

2. Symbols: Symbols are things imbued with meaning. They are the foundations for communication and all human behavior. They transmit meaning across time. What are the anchor symbols in a culture? What rituals are repetitively reenacted to reinforce a people group's perception of reality? Look individually and collectively. Observe master symbols—anchor symbols—revealed through ritual on the individual, family, community, and national levels. What rival symbols in the culture will contest symbols from the Bible? Just like a story has a teller and hearers, symbols are conveyed through the senses: sight, smell, touch, taste, and hearing.

3. Plot: To what degree do themes (unifying/opposing) comport with the biblical metanarrative? How do master narratives in the host culture

32. Babbie, *The Practice of Social Research*.

33. Component parts of "plot" in a style common in the West: Introduction/exposition, complication or crisis, climax, resolution, and new realization

compare and contrast with the biblical metanarrative? What will you do with what you know is truth from this story? What emotions are expressed?

4. Setting: In what ways do time and space comport with biblical narrative?

Step 5: Analyze Stories is a key step in the methodology of *strategic storytelling*. A great deal of help is provided from the social sciences. Contrast the acuity and detail involved in the step with current methodologies and their associated assumptions. If indeed the unique message of the Bible coupled with the work of the Holy Spirit pierce through the targeted culture, displace unbiblical core worldview assumptions along with their cultural manifestations, and divinely make clear the message of truth, then this step and others are completely unnecessary. Human agency is drastically dismissed. The rules of empirical social research and analysis do not apply.

CONCLUDING REFLECTIONS

These first five steps of the twelve-step methodology of *strategic storytelling* are essential for anyone interested in reducing communication noise. It really does not matter whether one is communicating within one's own culture or across cultures. The basic principles apply. Of the five, which may be the most important? We would suggest that a "being among the people" approach is first and foremost. Author and activist Parker Palmer writes, "Knowing of any sort is relational".[34]

The next chapter will address steps six through nine of *strategic storytelling*.

---

34. Palmer, *The Courage to Teach*, 54.

7

Examining a Solution

Steps 6–9

INTRODUCTORY REMARKS

THIS CHAPTER CONTINUES WITH the next steps in the methodology for *strategic storytelling*. Previously, in Chapter 6 we examined entering a culture, developing authentic relationships, and collecting essential social facts by observing and understanding symbols, stories, and rituals. Here in Chapter 7 we discover what to tell and how to tell it.

STEP 6: UNDERSTAND THE LOCAL METANARRATIVE

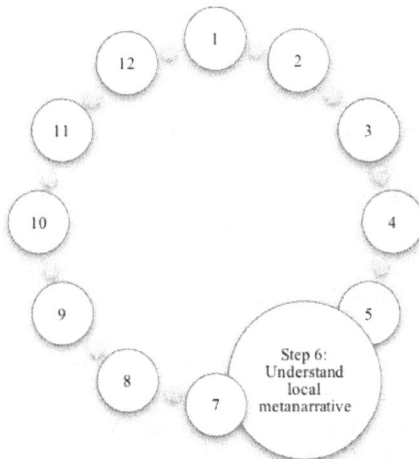

Figure 7.1: Metanarrative

In Step 4 the storyteller collects stories in the host society. Over time and through observation it becomes evident that all stories are not the same. A few emerge as dominant. As described in the previous chapter, some may meet criteria for master narratives. An example is the Pharaoh master narrative in Arabic Islam.

Single stories may cluster together into a set of stories. In Argentina, there are many individual stories about family members and friends who disappeared during the years of the Dirty War. All these stories together form a cluster of stories about the "disappeared ones". With one voice this cluster speaks about the atrocities committed by government officials.

Single stories and clusters of stories coalesce over time to form the metanarrative of a group of people. Obviously, there is no one metanarrative in Egypt or Argentina. But, among a homogeneous group of people there generally is an overarching story.

A *metanarrative* is the big picture story. It is comprehensive and supplies meaning to most, if not all, aspects of a culture's life. It orders events and explains experiences. A metanarrative is an overall framework. It is the total library. In other words, metanarrative is a function of discourse.

The prophet Isaiah describes the receptor dilemma faced by any person speaking on behalf of God into cultures. The dilemma is not new. According to the prophet, the impasse has existed from ancient times. The one who first demonstrates and then proclaims the good news of a Redeemer, the Lord of Hosts, does so into a context illustrated vividly in the following depiction from Isaiah 44 (ESV). Note how the local metanarrative has shaped the worldview of people. Then, based upon the worldview, one either sees what is true or does not. Below is the fuller text from Isaiah with emphasis added by the authors.

> Isaiah 44:9—20:9All who fashion idols are *nothing*, and the things they delight in *do not profit*. Their witnesses *neither see nor know*, that they may be put to shame. 10Who fashions a god or casts an idol that is *profitable for nothing*? 11Behold, all his companions shall be put to shame, and the craftsmen are *only human*. Let them all assemble, let them stand forth. They shall be terrified; they shall be *put to shame* together. 12The ironsmith takes a cutting tool and works it over the coals. He fashions it with hammers and works it with his strong arm. He becomes hungry, and his strength fails; he drinks no water and is faint. 13The carpenter stretches a line; he marks it out with a pencil. He shapes it with planes and marks it with a compass. He shapes it into the figure of a man, with the

beauty of a man, to dwell in a house. 14He cuts down cedars, or he chooses a cypress tree or an oak and lets it grow strong among the trees of the forest. He plants a cedar and the rain nourishes it. 15Then it becomes fuel for a man. He takes a part of it and warms himself; he kindles a fire and bakes bread. Also he *makes a god* and worships it; he makes it an idol and falls down before it. 16Half of it he burns in the fire. Over the half he eats meat; he roasts it and is satisfied. Also he warms himself and says, "Aha, I am warm, I have seen the fire!" 17And the rest of it he makes into a god, his idol, and falls down to it and worships it. He prays to it and says, "Deliver me, for you are my god!" 18*They know not, nor do they discern*, for he has *shut their eyes*, so that they cannot see, and their hearts, so that they cannot understand. 19No one considers, nor is there knowledge or discernment to say, "Half of it I burned in the fire; I also baked bread on its coals; I roasted meat and have eaten. And shall I make the rest of it an abomination? Shall I fall down before a block of wood?" 20He feeds on ashes; a deluded heart has led him astray, and he cannot deliver himself or say, "*Is there not a lie* in my right hand?" (ESV)[1]

The lengthy biblical text describes an idolatrous man, which in dramatic irony is a designation completely outside his own awareness.[2] He does not know he is an idolater. He is simply living out his life on the basis of the big picture story he knows and embraces. He is unable to say that the idol is a lie.[3] Ah, but the prophet from the outside sees and says the truth. He has the *etic* perspective.

1. The text of Isaiah 44 raises powerful questions. It suggests that idols are human creations. The idol is nothing. It has no power. What the misguided carpenter holds in his hand is a lie. The danger is not in the cypress or oak itself. Danger lies in the deception *associated* with the object. In other words, the risk resides in cognition rather than the physical realm.

2. Isaiah's Description of the Dilemma (note selected verses and accompanying expressions)—09 Neither see nor know, 10 Only human, 15 He makes a god and worships it, 15 He makes it an idol and falls down before it, 18 They know not, nor do they discern, 18 He has shut their eyes, so that they cannot see, 18 Their hearts, so that they cannot understand, 19 No one considers, nor is there knowledge, 20 A deluded heart has led him astray, 20 He cannot . . . say, "Is there not a lie in my right hand?"

3. Although Paul the Apostle asserts that Satan has blinded the minds of those who do not believe (2 Corinthians 4:4), the Apostle also forcefully implicates man himself (Romans 1–3). He says that men and women have chosen to believe the lie (Romans 1:25). And for that they are without excuse. They tell and retell each other a story that is not true. This is done over time. Stubbornly resistant, it seems culture cannot change.

The storyteller crafts the biblical story, knowing it is true and most as-suredly that it is a rival story to what already is told and retold in the host so-ciety. By knowing and understanding the local metanarrative, the storyteller is able to tell the story of God with intention and skill. He lays foundations, raises questions, artfully counters fabrications, and retells the story of reality.

STEP 7: CRAFT THE BIBLICAL STORY

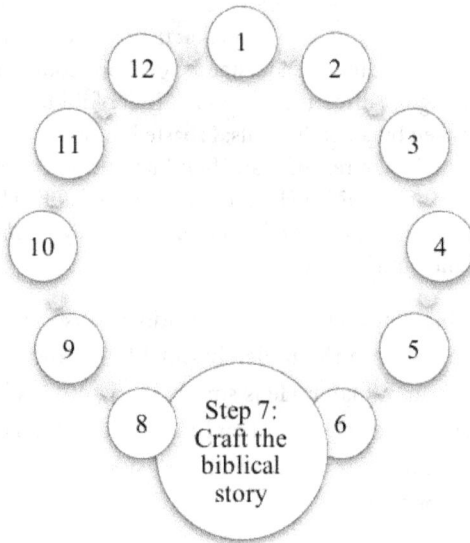

Figure 7.2: Craft the Biblical Story

At a minimum there are two metanarratives or collections of controlling stories. One has existed across time in the local culture. Just like worldview, the existing metanarrative may be outside the awareness of locals. Although tacitly assumed and embraced, it impacts all aspects of life.

It is into this context that the storyteller tells to teach the biblical metanarrative (see Figure 7.2). The biblical metanarrative becomes the rival story as it is told. Again, in dramatic irony, locals do not realize they already live in the biblical narrative but live out their lives as per a dissonant story. In this way the biblical narrative is not foreign. It is actually the story of the host society, but they do not know it.

So, as people hear and understand the rival story, both metanarratives co-exist. The old is not mystically displaced by the new. Yes, the former can be displaced and the existing worldview can be changed. But, like all efforts in rhetorical discourse, such change requires narration, description, exposition, and argumentation. Elaboration of the biblical narrative is rich in detail. It is planned. It recalls, describes, and expands. Its goal is a complex emergent whole. "Stories are the last frontier in a fight between worldviews".[4] Evangelist Leighton Ford puts it this way, "Conversion is a collision of narratives".[5]

There is an imperative to share the Gospel Story in the framework of the whole of the Christian Scriptures.[6] It is a simple story, but a story with deep roots in history. The message of the Gospel is the Storyline in the Sacred Storybook, a storybook that is God's metanarrative. Effective storytelling tells the whole story rather than starting in the middle of the story. Effective storytelling also tells the story in a manner whereby the hearers are struck with the indisputable fact that they are already in this story. Again, it is not foreign. It is their story.

Starting points can and should differ for specific audiences. Beginning with a proverb may appeal to some Muslims. David Parks' *Flashback* begins with what some audiences are familiar with, the New Testament.[7] He makes a point from the New Testament, and then flashes back to the Old Testament. He does this until the big picture is covered. Eventually, the cross-cultural worker will return to the metanarrative.

Consider the comments of missionary/linguist Fran Popovich, who worked among the Maxakali people of Brazil:

> I believe that the translation of the New Testament has not been adequate to reveal the whole counsel of God . . . Old Testament teachings are needed to show how God wants to be worshipped and invoked. They demonstrate graphically that God is vitally concerned with the mundane affairs of human beings. Much of what we find syncretistic in Maxakali practice we can attribute to an inadequate theology of God, one that the stories of Joseph, Moses, David, Elijah, Elisha, and Daniel would do much to remedy.[8]

---

4. Slack and Terry, *Chronological Bible Storying*, 34.

5. Ford, *The Power of Story*, 14.

6. Steffen and Terry, "The Sweeping Story of Scripture".

7. Parks, *Flashback*.

8. Popovich, "The Old Testament," 32–36.

In other words, the Old Testament narrative frames God as relevant to all the affairs of life. He is not only the High God, but also the Low God as well. The point is not to tell the top ten stories from the Bible, but to impart the metanarrative of God throughout the Bible, a metanarrative in which the hearer is already a character.

No doubt *strategic storytelling* is far more effective with concrete relational learners than is topical teaching. However, the authors do not see storytelling as a panacea. This one step, crafting the biblical story, cannot be removed from the accompanying eleven steps that comprise *strategic storytelling*. Alone, this one step is no remedy.

STEP 8: INTERNALIZE THE BIBLICAL STORY

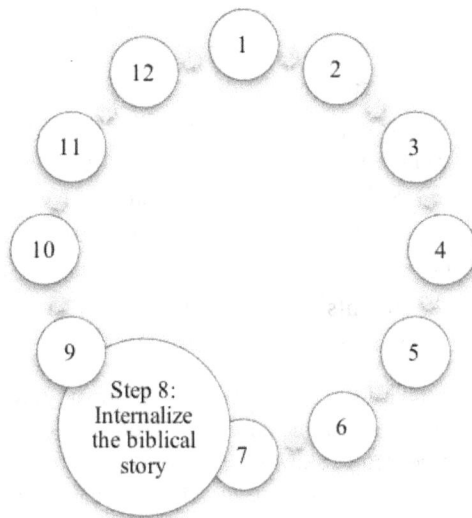

Figure 7.3: Internalize the Biblical Story

To internalize the biblical story, the cross-cultural worker does more than simply practice delivering it so that the presentation flows and makes sense. The presentation of the biblical story is not a one-time speech, perfected through practice. The storyteller must be intimately familiar with the whole story, each component part, and all the interrelationships.

Furthermore, the internalized biblical story means that the messenger is the message. He does not laud one story but live another. The message of the story itself has changed the messenger.

Because the messenger is "among the people," the people hearing the story also see the lived message over time. The criticality is not simply that the message is sound. It must also be visibly elaborated through lived experience.

STEP 9: TELL TO TEACH—T2T

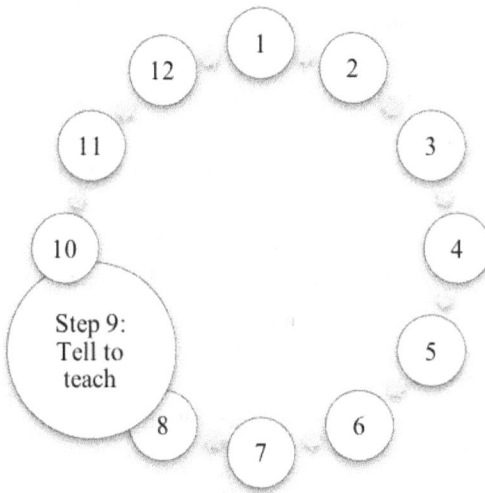

Figure 7.4: Tell to Teach

Strategic storytelling is predicated upon the assumption that simply telling a story is often ineffectual. But, expositional telling is effectual. The objective is to teach (. . . 2T or cause to learn) not simply to tell (*t* . . .). Again, coupled with the emphasis on cultural anthropology, telling to teach is a key fundamental difference between *strategic storytelling* and the existing methods in the orality movement. Empirical evidence has demonstrated the ineffectiveness of simply telling a story.

What is *t*2T? While recognizing the power of a story format, *strategic storytelling* does not see "story" as a cure-all for past maladies in cross-cultural communication. Together with story, language acquisition is required. Culture investigation is necessary. Trust bonds within authentic relationships must be developed.[9] The existing metanarrative and world-view should be challenged and deconstructed. A new metanarrative and worldview must be championed and constructed.

Table 7.1 highlights what we may have missed in past mission methods. Maladies have not been remedied simply by modifying the method of delivery from a topical approach to a story approach. The results remain largely the same.

Method	Result	Missing Missiological Methods	Method	Same Result
		Living among the people		
		Language proficiency Level 3 or 4 as per the Interagency Language Roundtable (ILR) scale		
		Culture research in precedent literature plus investigation "in the field" via reliable and valid approaches to inquiry		
		Authentic relationships in the host society		
		Trust bonds as the foundation to communication		
		Clear communication where decoding matches encoding because of culture and language acquisition		
Topical teaching	Syncretism	Modeling the story experientially to support its applicability and credibility	Story-telling	Syncretism
		Holistic message that addresses socio-cultural institutional structures and functions		
		A big picture story from Scripture as the rival metanarrative		
		Worldview confrontation		
		Differentiation between form, function, and meaning in critical contextualization		
		Discipleship and mentoring of emerging local leaders		
		Leadership development as exit strategy		
		Delegating responsibility		

Table 7.1: Whether Topical Teaching or Storytelling, Missing Missiological Methods

9. Mayers says the prior question of trust (PQT) simply asks, "Is what I am doing, thinking, and saying, building trust or undermining trust?" (Mayers, *Christianity Confronts Culture*, 7).

Table 7.1 highlights fourteen often missed missiological methods. There indeed may be more. The authors in this series argue that these methods are not magically remitted by fiat sovereignty (see Steffen, Tom. "Flawed Evangelism and Church Planting." *Evangelical Missions Quarterly* 34 (1998) 428–35.). Each method is rooted in anthropology. Each represents an actual and factual function in human exchange. God made man in human relationships with functional norms.[10]

Telling a story is not a soliloquy. Story involves teller and hearer. Likely, the exchange is interactive. But, interaction may not take place easily in a socially stratified society. Story has component parts including but not limited to the storyline, characters, and setting. The oratory ability of the teller is key.

To be clear, the *strategic storytelling* methodology may be more powerful than topical teaching, particularly among concrete relational learners. But, it is not all-powerful. It does not automatically carry out the activities listed in the table above in the column "Missing Missiological Methods". If the missing methods are absent in strategic storytelling, their absence will thwart communication in the same way their absence impedes topical teaching.

So, the emphasis of Step 9: Tell to Teach—t2T is that storytelling must be combined with exposition along with proven missiological methods.

---

10. Fourteen Features of Strategic Storytelling (note emphasis): (a) Focuses on *the process of learning* rather than simply covering content, (b) Encourages learner *proactivity* rather than passivity, (c) Promotes *exploration and contextualization* rather than memorization, (d) Progresses from *whole to part*, (e) Evaluates the learning *experience* as well as its content, (f) In time and as culturally appropriate, develops *interactive engagement* rather than lectures, (g) Communication is more of a *dialogue* rather than a monologue, (h) Honors formality as culturally required but encourages informality as a learning strategy, (i) Maintains respect as culturally necessary but authorizes questions, (j) *Applies* curricular content versus mere abstract conceptualization, (k) *Holistic*, addressing cognition, affect, and psycho-motor skills rather than only dispensing knowledge, (l) Designs learning activities that are *experiential*, (m) Learning by doing and being as well as hearing, (n) Is aware of the core assumptions in the West that may not be shared globally: self-effort vs. fate, change as positive vs. negative, equality vs. hierarchical, induction vs. deduction, guilt/innocence vs. shame/honor pattern of culture, individualism vs. group orientation, abstract vs. concrete learners, andragogy vs. pedagogy, exposure vs. concealment of vulnerability, direct vs. indirect communication

CONCLUDING REFLECTIONS

Far beyond simply sharing symbol or story bits as an outsider without historical precedence, the equipped and prepared storyteller in *strategic storytelling* understands the big picture narrative in the locale, models the life and love of the Lord Jesus through lived experiences "among the people", and tells to teach the Good News in its totality as a rival metanarrative.

The next chapter will describe the final steps in the methodology.

8

Examining a Solution

Steps 10–12

INTRODUCTORY REMARKS

THIS CHAPTER CONTINUES WITH the final steps in the methodology of *strategic storytelling*. Previously Chapter 7 examined what to tell and how to tell it. That chapter stressed the importance of crafting and telling the biblical story as a rival metanarrative. Here in Chapter 8 we evaluate outcomes. Was meaning transferred? Did authentic conversion take place? Were new leaders developed? Was the region transformed? So, Step 10 details the theory and processes of effective communication as a foundation to validate if meaning transfer occurs (see Figure 8.1).

STEP 10: VALIDATE MEANING

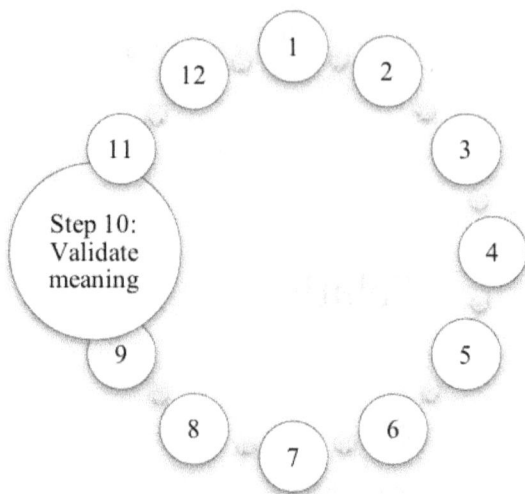

Figure 8.1: Validate Meaning

A basic assumption in effective communication is that a receiver decodes a message to an expected degree of correspondence to what the sender encodes. If this decoding/encoding process is successful, then effective communication takes place. The imagery that follows in Figure 8.2 shows the overall process of communication adapted from the research of Claude Shannon (1949).[1] In the imagery below and the accompanying fictitious narrative, an elderly woman from the north of India goes as a patient to a team of German physicians.

---

1. Of course, since 1949, others have added to the theory of communication, notably Robert T. Craig, communication theorist at the University of Colorado, Boulder, Colorado. However, often the original model by Claude Shannon is used to lay a foundation for communication theory.

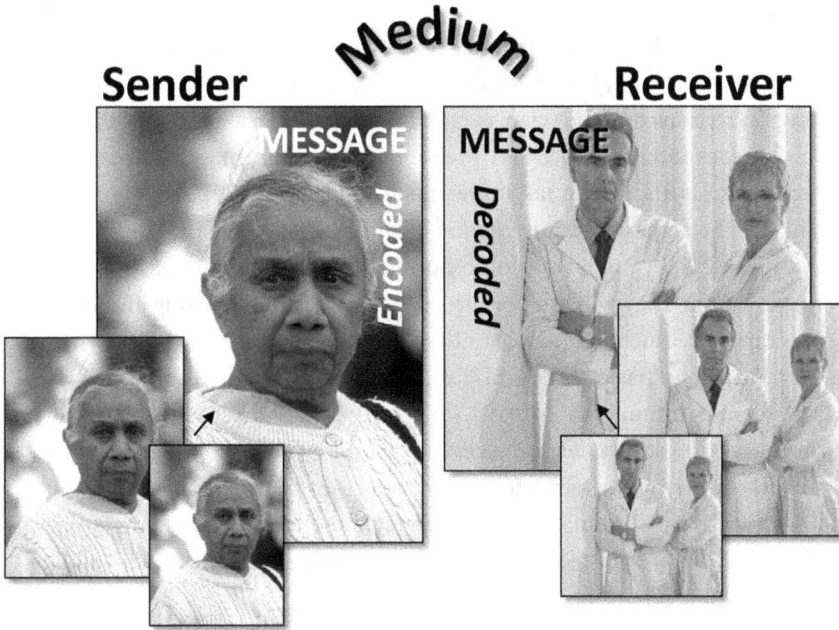

Figure 8.2: Model of Communication

The sender is from a Hindu background. She and her husband are from the Vaisya community of business entrepreneurs. They immigrated to Germany from New Delhi, the capital of India, three years ago in order to be close to their son, an entrepreneur in Frankfurt. She speaks Hindi, Punjabi, and Anglo-English. She is slowly learning German. She is devout in her Hindu faith and practice, even more so since moving to Europe.

Although she may not openly talk about impersonal spiritual forces, she tacitly assumes they exist and impact every aspect of her life. Her husband has stopped the puja practice in their apartment, and she suspects this lapse is somehow related to the pain she feels in her stomach. In fact, she is quite sure of it. Yet, she is hesitant to speak directly. She has even wondered, if she says anything about her stomach pain, whether the doctors will think she is speaking negatively of German food. What will she say to the physicians? She has decided that she will take her time and allow a relationship to evolve. She will speak as best she can in English. Based upon her hierarchal upbringing, she knows they are the experts.

The receivers are German-born medical doctors who have practiced general medicine in Frankfurt for many years. They speak German and

English. Neither was raised in any religion and both are secular through and through. They do not believe in personal spirit beings or impersonal spiritual forces. They are materialists. They speak directly without speculation. They know that the scientific method of empirical research is the only valid means to know what they know. Of course, they have had many patients from India, but do not know much at all about Hinduism, animism, and life throughout the vast nation of India. What will they hear when she speaks? They are busy and do not have much if any time for personal conversation. They will ask her directly what she feels is wrong and let her participate as much as possible in the diagnosis process.

Shannon's basic theory of communication highlights the locations where miscommunication likely may occur: the background biases and preconceptions of sender and receiver, encoding and decoding of meaning, skill in conveying the message, and all aspects of the medium.

Effective communication is rarely attained in haste. It requires time. What are the proven techniques from communication theory to validate meaning transfer? Consider the following:

1. Never assume anything. If you must assume something, assume that communication has not taken place.

	CHECKLIST (order of priority)	✓
1	Common language	
2	Culture general and specific knowledge	
3	Relationship	
4	Trust	
5	Accommodating environment	
6	Symbols identified and defined	
7	Story-defined key terms and concepts	
8	Storytelling style contextualized	
9	Able to retell big picture story	
10	Communication goal(s) exploited	

Table 8.1: Communication Checklist

2. Look first and foremost at the medium. This element in the process of communication is the key. Is the message communicated in a commonly understand language? Always recognize that culture and language are inseparable. What is the relationship between sender and receiver? Is there trust? Is the environment of communication accommodating? Related to environment, are basic humans needs as per Maslow's hierarchy being meet? All these factors are part of medium.

3. Identify key terms and concepts. Define these through shared stories rather than direct inquiry. As component parts are put into place, a whole will materialize. Communicate whole to part, but validate part to whole. This step of validation relates to encoding and decoding. As to story solicitation, being explicit may be disrespectful in high context cultures, in which one cannot ask direct questions to validate meaning. A sender must adapt the degree of explicitness or implicitness to the cultural norm. Solicit response in the form of story[2].

4. Story styles vary across cultures. See Anne Pellowski's (1990) *The World of Storytelling*. The medium is the message; therefore, the story must be crafted and shared in a contextualized way that is locally familiar.

5. What is the overall story the hearer is able to retell? What symbols caught their attention?

6. Pay attention to different goals in communication. Note the acronym, *TRIP*: topic, relationships, identity, and process (see Figure 8.3). A U.S. American may want to stick to the *topic*. Friends from Latin America will focus on *relationship* in communication more so than specific topics. Throughout Asia it is critical to be aware of *identity* in human exchange. In such environments, power distance is a critical factor. German physicians may sense the importance of *process*. A skilled storyteller is able to adapt to the communication goal of the hearer, building out the story plot on that foundation.

2. In group-oriented societies where people relate to one another through a shame/honor pattern, it is seldom useful to ask direct questions. Despite the venerable work of James Spradley (1979) in *The Ethnographic Interview*, asking direct questions may work in a Western context, but it is not useful in many cross-cultural settings.

| Topic | Relationship | Identity | Process |

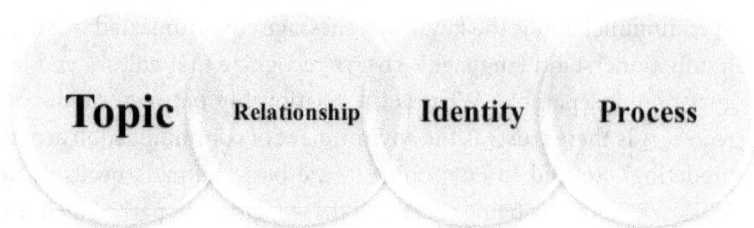

Figure 8.3: Communication Goals

Finally, what is the storyteller validating? If one is to validate meaning transfer, what is "meaning" and how is it measured? *Meaning* refers to the encoded and decoded message. What is intended by the sender and inferred by the receiver?

Don Kirkpatrick argues that there are four levels of "meaning" evaluation represented in four simple questions.[3]

1. Do they like it?

2. Do they get it?

3. Can they do it?

4. Did it make a difference?

Do they like it? This question relates to the affective domain of learning, the most important factor in teaching. For the cross-cultural worker, the affective domain has to do with the feelings developed in authentic relationships with people. From these friendships, trust is built that becomes the foundation for the credibility of the message.

Do they get it? This question relates to cognition. Benjamin Bloom (1913–1999) created a taxonomy of learning that helps the instructor understand the ascending levels of cognition.[4] At an elementary level, learners *know* terminology and *comprehend* definitions. At an intermediate level, learners are able to *apply* what they know and comprehend to real life situ-

3. These levels of evaluation are adapted from the work of Don Kirkpatrick (2006) in *Evaluating Training Programs*. Kirkpatrick is a communication expert, past President of the American Society for Training and Development (ASTD), and a senior elder at Elmbrook Church in Brookfield, Wisconsin.

4. Bloom's Taxonomy of Cognitive Learning (six levels): Knowledge, Comprehension, Application, Analysis, Synthesis, Transfer (Bloom originally referred to this stage as "evaluation")

ations. Then, at the most advanced level, higher order-learning means the hearer is able to see the component parts of the whole through *analysis*, put all the component parts back together through *synthesis*, and *transfer* what is known and comprehended in one discipline to a brand new area of inquiry.

Educators have compiled lists of action verbs that correlate to each stage of cognitive learning. These action verbs can help the storyteller validate what the hearer does and does not understand. Furthermore, educators have identified artifacts and learning activities that befit each stage. Figure 8.4 provides a detailed analysis of Bloom's "Taxonomy of Cognitive Learning".

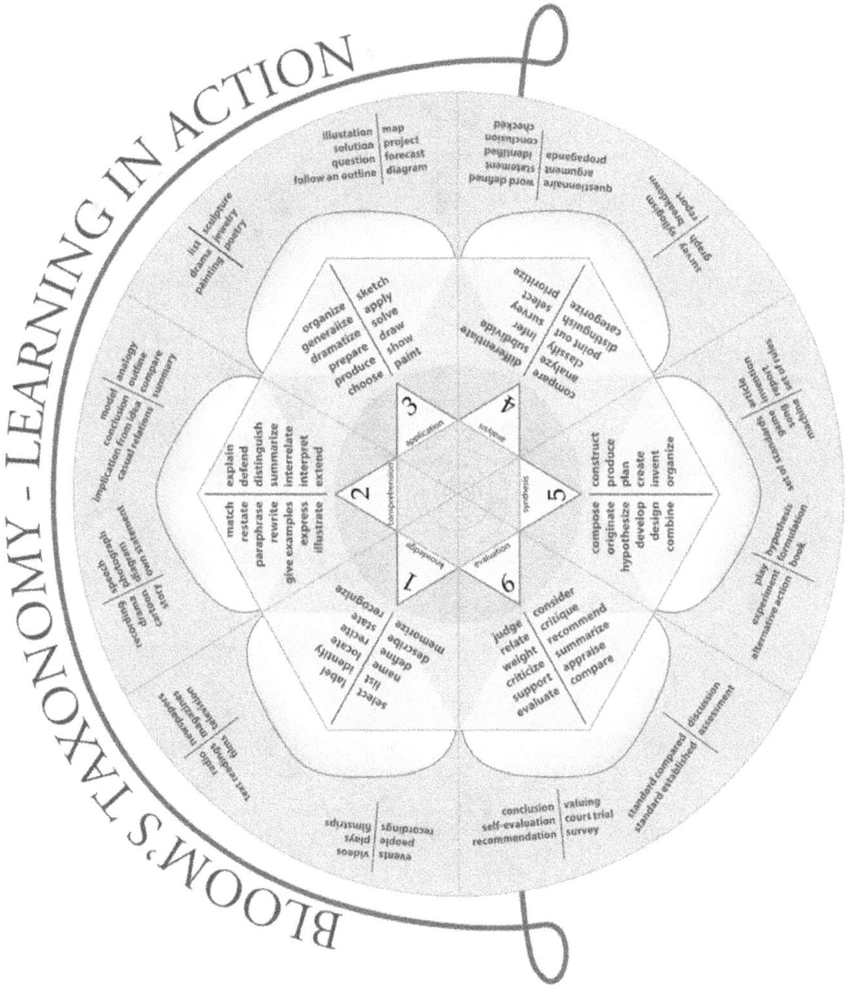

Figure 8.4: Bloom's Taxonomy Rose

Can they do it? This question relates to skills. Is the story hearer able to embrace the biblical metanarrative and its component stories? Does he change his mind about what is and is not real, what ought and ought not to be, cause and effect, how he relates to Other, and what is and is not said and done? Beyond simply adding new behaviors to his pattern of life, does he correspondingly stop saying and doing what were normal to the old ways but now are known to be in opposition to the nature and character of the God of the Bible? Note that a big picture view, an overall way of living, is far more important than isolated behaviors.

Figure 8.5: White Puzzle

Figure 8.6: Black Puzzle

If two jigsaw puzzles could illustrative metanarratives, consider the following. Imagine that a white puzzle (see Figure 8.5) represents the biblical metanarrative and a black puzzle (see Figure 8.6) represents the "old ways," as Hiebert and his coauthors called them. Revelation 21:4 refers to them as "the old order of things" (NIV). In cultures there may or may not be overlapping assumptions, values, institutions, and behaviors common to both metanarratives. But, as comprehensive systems, the old ways and the biblical metanarrative are not the same and are not compatible as systems. If a story hearer takes a puzzle piece from the white puzzle, that is, a single symbol or mere story bit from the overall biblical metanarrative, and attempts to incorporate it into the black puzzle, this is syncretism. It is unnatural. In truth it does not fit. If this type of behavioral activity and others like it that represent miscommunication are not arrested, the activities build a corridor directly toward Christo-paganism. Left unobstructed, such indiscriminate mixing of new and old will create a discordant cacophony of confusion (see Figure 8.7).

Figure 8.7: Indiscriminate Mix of New and Old

Rather than a mere theoretical postulation, such confusion is rampant in the global church. We do not fault the hearers but the storytellers. Story has replaced topical teaching as a best practice in missions, but in reality there has been little change of the core methodology of communication and therefore little improvement in the capability to transfer meaning.

Recently the wife of a prominent Christian leader among a people group in Western Canada told me she is terrified of the spirit world. She confided that the stories of spirits she heard from her grandmother still ring true in her mind and heart. In other words, the black puzzle as a whole has never been displaced. As recent, a local church pastor from South Asia told me that several of his parishioners mentioned to him that the illnesses his family was experiencing likely had been caused by the evil eye.

Does it make a difference? This is the fourth of Kirkpatrick's levels of evaluation. Ultimately, telling to teach ($t2T$) the biblical metanarrative must make a difference in the community, family, and individual.

Finally, when considering the step of validating meaning, we must recognize that communication is not always effective. At times, and perhaps often, it fails. Consider these examples from the Bible:

Sender	Receiver	Text	Message	Results
God	Adam	Gen 2:17	Do not eat from the tree of the knowledge of good and evil.	Adam and Eve disobeyed God and ate the fruit (Gen 3:6).
Noah	Human race before the flood	2 Pet 2:5	Noah is described as a "preacher of righteousness."	Great wickedness (Gen 6:5); corrupt/full of violence (v. 11).
Moses	Israelites	Exod 6:9	God will deliver you from Egyptian slavery.	Israelites did not listen.
Moses/Aaron	Pharaoh	Exod 7–14	Release Israelites from slavery.	Pharaoh did not listen (7:4, 13, 16, 22; 8:15, 19; 9:12; 11:9).
Judges	Israelites	Judg 2:17	Repeated experiential delivery from enemies.	Israelites did not listen.
Prophets	Israelites	Neh 9:30	Text says God's Spirit through the prophets warned the Israelites over many years.	Israelites paid no attention.
Jeremiah	Israelites	Jer 1:17–19	God's pending judgment.	Israelites fought against him and his message.
Ezekiel	Israelites	Ezek 2–3	God's total sovereignty.	The house of Israel is not willing to listen (3:7).
Jesus	Pharisees	John 8	Jesus's message was validated through His own qualifications and the Father's authentication.	Religious leaders did not understand (8:27) but many put their faith in Him (8:30).
Stephen	Jewish Sanhedrin	Acts 7	Chronological story-based foundation for Christ.	Verses 57–58 say they covered their ears, yelled at the top of their voices, all rushed at him, dragged him out of the city, and stoned him to death.
Paul	Jewish leaders	Acts 28	The Kingdom of God and identity of Jesus.	Some were convinced but others disbelieved (28:23–24).

Table 8.2: Biblical examples of failed communication

Evaluation of meaning transfer must ultimately look beyond individuals and families to broader communities and regions.

STEP 11: TRAIN NEW STORYTELLERS

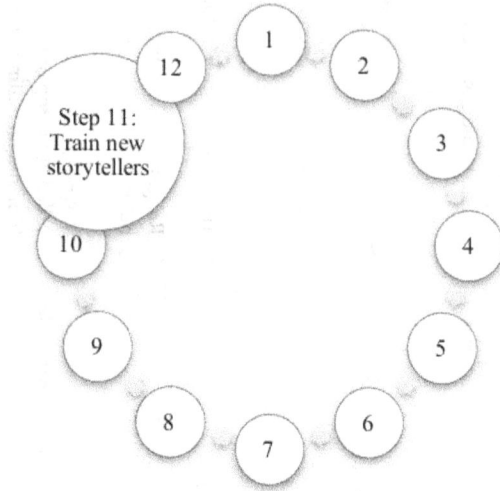

Figure 8.8: Train Storytellers

Strategic storytelling recognizes that in the New Testament model, local leaders lead local churches. They are the first objective in discipleship. The Greek term *ekklesia* predominately (112 times) refers to a community of Christ followers.[5] There are no clear-cut guidelines for admission into a local church. Apparently one would belong to a local church through living in a given locale, attending regularly, and participating. Other than Christ the head (Ephesians 1:22–23; 5:23–24), there are no indications in Scripture that additional offices exist in the universal church. But, the New Testament does describe roles and responsibilities in local churches. Table 8.3 analyzes local church leadership:

So, analysis of the data in the table above tells us a number of things about the roles and responsibilities of local church leadership.

---

5. Additionally, *ekklesia* is used to refer to a public assembly in the city of Ephesus (Acts 19:39), Israel (Acts 7:38), and a riotous mob (Acts 19:32, 41).

Local Church Leaders

Greek	Presbuteros	Presbuterion	Episkopos	Poimen	Diakonos
English	Elder	Presbytery	Bishop	Pastors	Deacon
References	Acts 14:23 Titus 1:5 1 Peter 5:1–2	1 Timothy 4:14	Acts 20:28 Philippians 1:1 1 Timothy 3:1–2 Titus 1:7	Ephesians 4:11	Acts 6:1–6 1 Timothy 3:8–13 Romans 16:1
Description	"Elder" is the most common term used in the New Testament and grammatically is always plural.	The "presbytery" of a local church is responsible to lead (Hebrews 13:7), oversee (Acts 20:28), teach (2 Timothy 2:2), and shepherd (1 Peter 5:2).	The Greek word is also translated "overseers". Always found in the plural.	The Greek word is commonly translated "shepherd", but there is one occurrence as "pastors" in the KJV.	The Greek term is commonly translated "servant".
Tradition	Terminology and practice are familiar to Presbyterian denominations. Some Presbyterian churches call the plurality of elders, the "session" (Latin, *sessio* from *sedere* "to sit"). In modern practice, a regional body of leaders is referred to as the "presbytery".		Note the Episcopal and Methodist traditions.	"Pastor" is the most commonly used term in North America despite its limited use in the New Testament.	The position is part of local church polity in Baptist and Presbyterian traditions.
Use of Terms	These four terms are synonymous in the New Testament. "Elders" and "presbytery" are English translations from the same Greek word. "Elders" and "bishops" are used interchangeably in Acts 20 to refer to the Ephesian church leaders ("elders" in v. 17, then "overseers" in vs. 28). Also, in 1 Peter 5:2 "elders" are instructed to take the oversight of the flock of God. In Titus 1:5–8, "elders" and "overseers" are used interchangeably. Finally, in 1 Peter 5:1–2 "elders" are exhorted to shepherd ("pastor") the flock of God.				The role seems to relate to the ministry of meeting physical needs of people.
Analysis	Throughout the New Testament the leadership of a local church is plural. There are always multiple pastors and deacons (Acts 14:23; 15:2,4,6,22,23; 20:17; 21:18; Philippians 1:1; Ephesians 4:11; 1 Thessalonians 5:12–13; 1 Timothy 4:14, 5:17; Titus 1:5; Hebrews 13:7,17,24; James 5:14; 1 Peter 5:1–2). They are always chosen from among the local community (Acts 14:21–25; Titus 1:5), never brought in from afar. They are homegrown. Specific qualifications are described in the New Testament for elders (1 Timothy 3:1–7; Titus 1:6–8) and deacons (Acts 6:2–4; 1 Timothy 3:8–13).				

Table 8.3: Analysis of Local Church Leaders

1. There is a biblical basis for leadership in a local church. This does not mean that leaders may "lord it over" congregants (Matthew 20:25, 1 Peter 5:3) but neither does it mean that the management model of the local church is flat, like a self-directed work team. Discipleship first focuses on leadership.

2. Roles of elders and deacons are differentiated.

3. Responsibilities are sketched out in Scripture. They are substantial and sobering.

4. Qualifications are certain and serious. The Scripture is clear that it is improper to hastily appoint people into these roles without clear demonstration of qualifications (1 Timothy 5:22). There must be functional competency displayed by a prospective leader over a period of time before entrusting the lives of men, women, and children to the authority of an elder or deacon.

5. The model of the Apostle Paul in the New Testament is instructive. He planted churches, discipled prospective leaders (Acts 20:28), and devoted months and years to assure fledgling churches were stabilized. The Epistles were part of his follow-up attention to church growth.

6. Local church leadership is accountable first and foremost to God but also to followers of Christ in the local community.

Training new storytellers goes far beyond short practice sessions of telling randomly selected Bible stories.[6] *Strategic storytelling* comprehends the step of training storytellers to be months and perhaps years of:

- Collaboration with local followers of Christ.

- Identification of potential leaders. Are you *t2T* the right people?

- Cultivation of spiritual qualities.[7]

6. For detailed explanations about designing training across cultures, see these resources: Robert Strauss. "Tribal Church Planter Profile." *International Journal of Frontier Missions* 15 (April–June 1998) 87–89. See also Robert Strauss. "Case Study of New Tribes Integral Training Program." In *Integral Ministry Training—Design and Evaluation*, edited by Robert Brynjolfson and Jonathan Lewis, 178–83. Pasadena, CA: WEA-William Carey Library, 2006. For the same explanation in Spanish, see Robert Strauss. "Fundamentos Para Guiar el Diseño de la Capacitación." Traducido por Yamina Gava y Barbara Compañy. In *Manual de Capacitación Transcultural: Una Guía Orientadora Los Procesos de Capacitación Misionera Integral*, edited by Omar Gava and Robert Strauss, 41–63. Villa Carlos Paz, Argentina: Recursos Estratégicos Globales, 2009.

7. Research shows these are universal (Worldview Resource Group, 2002 to 2008).

- Development of ministry capabilities.

- Transformation of the corporate community of Christ followers in new values, contextualized socio-cultural institutions, and God-honoring behavior.

- Localization of theology, strategy, and methodology.

- Mitigation of conflict.

- Transfer of authority, responsibility, and accountability to local leadership.

STEP 12: REACH THE STORYLAND

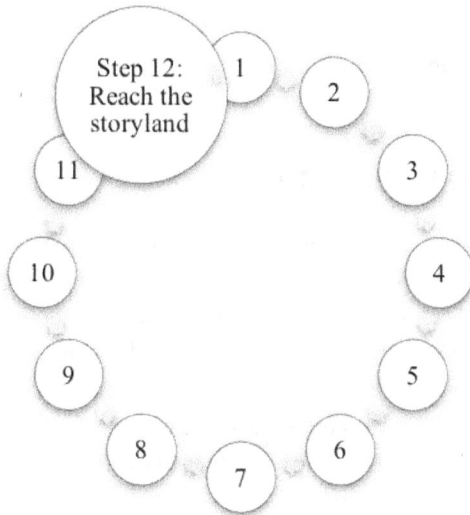

Figure 8.9: Reach the Storyland

The ultimate goal of ministry is that men, women, and children in a geographic region have had a valid opportunity to enter into a relationship with God, wherein they enjoy him and whereby he is gloried. Consider these attributes and activities of the missional church:

1. A local community of Christ followers who are beginning to display Kingdom values in everyday life (the church glorifies the Lord Jesus Christ and points to the "already, not yet" Kingdom of God).

2. Engaging people within social settings (an incarnational model) rather than separating from human culture (an extractional model).[8]

3. Rather than attracting people as consumers (come and see) to an institutionalized church through programs, *strategic storytelling* reaches the storyland through equipping followers of Christ to go out (go and be) into the local community to build relationships, serve, demonstrate, and proclaim.

4. It is God's mission to call people into a reconciled relationship with Him. "It is not so much that God has a mission for his church in the world, but that God has a church for his mission in the world".[9]

5. Simply telling a story to an individual in our community is insufficient. Words require works. The story of the Gospel must be embodied in a local community and accompanied by service that supports its credibility.

6. Programs support people on mission.

CONCLUDING REFLECTIONS

The nature of the problem often determines the approach of communication. If a house is on fire with all lives in danger, what is needed? Obviously, concise crystal clear information and loud hasty statements. "Wake up!" "There is a fire upstairs!" "Get out!" "Now!" The situation is not complicated. Social status is not a factor. Building relationships is completely unnecessary. There is no time. People and pets will die. The setting is a place of life-threatening danger. The only remedy is to escape as quickly as possible. "Hurry!"

What if the nature of the problem were as desperate as a house on fire, but the context did not permit haste, brevity, and mere bits of

---

8. A missional community of Christ followers does not neglect the spiritual and ministerial development of people. Megan works as a barista at a local Starbucks near my home, has a certification in sign language, and though somewhat interested is not yet a follower of Christ. Michael told her all she needed to do was love God. She responded, "That's it!" "Yes", he replied, "God will see that your love for Him is different from the evil all around you in other people. Because of that he will let you into heaven." Proverbs 26:10 says, "Like an archer who wounds as random is he who hires a fool or any passer-by" (NIV). Being missional does not justify a lack of skill.

9. Wright, *The New Testament and the People of God*, 62.

communication? Such is the case in most cross-cultural ministry. Men, women, and children who are not in relationship with God are in a desperate condition. But the context is not the same as a house fire, and the context matters.

In keeping with the metaphor, men, women, and children do not know the house is on fire. They do not know (eternal) death is close. They do not know you; you are a stranger in their house. They do not understand your unimportant nattering . . . it seems strange, as do you. Your talk of fire and your definitions are unfamiliar. Parents tell their children to stay away from you. Over time, you realize that you cannot be brief and should not speak hastily. Short, unconnected bits of information about burning houses and the danger of fire will not work. An entire big picture story about fire, its potency, danger, and mitigation is needed. Your master narrative of "the house is on fire" is at odds with existing anchor symbols and stories about safety and security. What is there already, the view of the world, is accepted. What you are saying is not.

Given the imperative to carry out ministry in the cross-cultural setting at a worldview level, we propose a methodology of *strategic storytelling*. There is a chronology and procedure to the method. It includes twelve steps that are carried out systematically over time and amidst genuine relationships. These steps address deep level worldview assumptions. It is possible to warn people and share good news with them.

You and I may be similar to the German physicians depicted in Figure 8.2. In normal circumstances we may be eminently qualified. However, in the cross-cultural setting we will need to add to our repertoire of skills.

In the next chapter, the authors reflect on the suggested solution and analyze its underlying philosophy and theology.

9

Analyzing a Solution

INTRODUCTORY REMARKS

ONE HUNDRED AND FIFTY years ago settlers moved along the Oregon Trail heading west into the American wilderness, struggling to survive harsh land and weather. Words of advice trickled back to those who followed: "Beware of shortcuts".[1]

Today there is an urgency to carry the words of life out into frontiers where men, women, and children are lost. Nevertheless, it behooves us to heed this warning. Even if we do not agree, at least we should be clear as to why. Just any path will not do for the journey. Some paths are beset with danger. Other paths are safer.

This chapter attempts to make clear the assumptions that drive *strategic storytelling*.

ASSUMPTIONS RELATED TO STRATEGIC STORYTELLING

What are underlying philosophical and theological assumptions of *strategic storytelling* and its vital communication feature, telling-to-Teach (*t2T*)? Here we will look through the same five grids as Chapter 3 but will add one more, related to the storyteller (see Figure 9.1).

---

1. See *The Oregon Trail*, Frances Parkman, 2008.

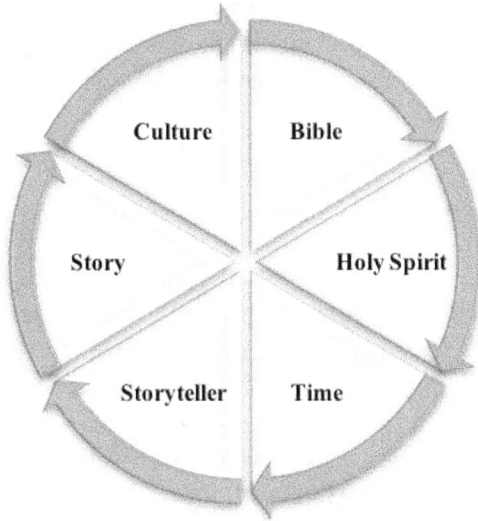

Figure 9.1: Six Grids of Analysis

1. RELATED TO THE BIBLE

1.1 The efficacy of the biblical story is its message of salvation history.

Scripture is replete with descriptions of the effectual ability of God's Word. The truth of God shared throughout the storyline of Scripture reveals God, the Protagonist of the Story, and his way for humankind to restore a relationship with him. The truth is piercing to all and comforting to many. Through it we understand the way back to him.

Storytelling tenets inform us that God's story is pulling us in ... drawing us to him.[2] Scripture teaches us that the Holy Spirit is also drawing us toward God (John 6:44; 12:32), away from our natural bent to depart from and deny him (Romans 1–3).

Strategic storytelling makes a distinction between the truth revealed in the words of the Holy Scriptures and the written/oral speaking of those words. It is not in the vocal vibrations or "streams of sound," as linguist and translator Kathleen Callow calls them, where efficacy is found.[3] Po-

2. See *The Story Factor*, 2006, by Annette Simmons.

3. Callow, *Man and Message*, 3.

tency is in the meaning of those words. At one point Peter told Jesus, "You have the words of eternal life" (John 6:68). It is in this way that we assume, philosophically and theologically, that the Bible is powerful. In it salvation history is revealed.

1.2 The effectiveness of the biblical story is tied to telling/teaching.

Furthermore, the efficacy of the salvation history plot depends upon the processes of calling, sending, telling, hearing, understanding, and responding appropriately (Romans 10:13–15). Further, the "telling" of Romans 10 is made effectual through procedures of teaching, reproof, correction, and training (1 Timothy 3:16). Overall these processes and procedures, ordained by God, are the means by which one becomes a comprehensively equipped and fit follower of God.

In the realm of organizational training, business consultants Harold Stolovitch and Erica Keeps have taught us similarly through their research-based book, *Telling Ain't Training*. In the first chapter, they improve their grammar and say, "Learning is not easy".[4] Any student of the Gospels knows this all too clearly. The Gospel of Mark particularly and unmistakably presents the disciples as actually being dull in their understanding of Jesus' teaching about the Passion (Mark 8–10). Even at the end of Jesus' earthly ministry, they still ask if this whole thing is about the restoration of the political reign of the Jewish nation (Acts 1:6), a common presupposition in Judaism about the earthly Messiah.[5]

---

4. Stolovitch and Keeps, *Telling Ain't Training*, 3.

5. It was commonplace in Hebrew thought that the Messiah would be ordained by God, a human descendant of David, well versed in Mosaic Law, and a mighty political and military leader. But, there was no common expectation that he would be divine. It must have been quite strange in Mark 11 when Jesus entered Jerusalem as a humble Rabbi riding on the foal of a donkey (Zechariah 9:9). He did not enter riding on a white horse of war (Revelation 19:14). He did not go to the Roman military garrison housed within the colonnades of the Antonia Fortress. He went straight to the Temple and cleansed it. What was His first concern upon arrival at the Temple? He was incensed that the Court of the Gentiles had been set up for entrepreneurial trade, thereby excluding Gentiles from approaching God in worship. Rather than attacking the Roman Empire, Jesus attacked the religious system of the Jews.

1.3 The meaning of the biblical story is distorted by an existing network of core worldview assumptions.

Perhaps there is no better illustration than Jesus' disciples. The story of God recorded in the Bible collides with existing rival stories (also known by the term *culture*) in a host society. The historical narrative of the Gospels tells us that Jesus shared with his disciples in Caesarea Philippi that He would go to Jerusalem and suffer death (Mark 8). Six days later after the Transfiguration of Jesus on Mount Tabor (Mark 9), where Elijah and Moses discussed God's plan that Jesus would journey to Jerusalem to die (Luke 15), the disciples still did not understand and, in fact, began to debate among themselves who would be greater in the coming political kingdom.

At the very moment that Jesus was speaking privately to the disciples about the betrayal, death, and resurrection of the Son of Man, James and John came to Him asking if they particularly, out from the other disciples, could sit on Jesus' right hand when He set up His throne and reign as King in Jerusalem (Mark 10).

Amidst the collision of rival stories with all their associated assumptions and expectations, the Bible is rejected, accommodated, or assimilated based upon innumerable factors. "Just telling Bible stories does not guarantee Bible meaning".[6] Jesus, the ultimate storyteller, knew this. Telling "ain't" training. The Apostle Paul told Timothy the same, that meaning transfer requires teaching, reproof, correction, and training.

1.4 An accurate understanding of the biblical story is directly related to intentionality.

As to the perspicuity of Scripture, theologian Grant Osborne writes, "Scripture does not automatically cross cultural barriers to impart its meaning. We know that God does not miraculously reveal the meaning of passages whenever they are read".[7] In his award-willing book *The Hermeneutical Spiral: A Complete Introduction to Biblical Interpretation*, Osborne devotes almost 500 pages to explain how meaning is created. It is created through a detailed process of interpretation.

Leland Ryken concurs in *Words of Delight: A Literary Introduction to the Bible*, also a book of over 500 pages:

6. Steffen, *The Facilitator Era*, 138.

7. Osborne, *The Hermeneutical Spiral*, 7.

The prime literary rule of interpretation is *meaning through form*. Any complete understanding of a story depends on our ability to formulate the intellectual truth of the story as well—not as a substitute for the imaged reality of the settings, characters, and events, but as an interpretive lens through which we see their significance. All of this is a way of saying that we need a *methodology* for getting from the story to the theme—from setting, character, and plot to an *intellectual grasp of what the story is about and the perspective that the writer expects* us to take toward that subject.[8] (emphasis added)

Yes, there is a methodology to "telling" the biblical story. In other words, there is more to telling the story than simply telling the story. Osborne and Ryken did not write in vain. We embrace the rigor they describe. In the Book of Acts, the Ethiopian recognized this same need as he read the prophet Isaiah. When Philip asked, "Do you understand?" the Ethiopian replied, "How can I unless I have someone to guide me?" (Acts 8:30–38). Philip the Evangelist was called, sent, and told. The Ethiopian heard, understood, and responded appropriately.[9]

1.5 The primary characteristic of the biblical story is the feature of biblical theology.

Biblical and systematic theologies are frequently contrasted, primarily for two reasons: their structure and purposes differ. "In contrast to systematic theology, which categorizes doctrine according to specific topics, biblical theology shows the unfolding of God's revelation as it progressed through history".[10]

The important feature of biblical theology is the disclosing of divine truth embedded in a historical narrative over an extended period of time.[11] Not everything is revealed at once to any one person. And it is the full story that unveils the complete picture of God.[12]

---

8. Ryken, *Words of Delight*, 81.

9. To clarify, these assumptions about the Bible do not support Karl Barth's view that the Bible is limited to "instrumental authority" that is, that its function as a fallible human work is only to point us to the divinely revealed Christ. Contrarily, we view Scripture as infallible, divinely inspired, and having absolute authority.

10. Gotquestions.org; see also Beale, *A New Testament Biblical Theology*.

11. Walker, *Progressive Revelation*.

12. Looking more closely at biblical theology, there may be different types depending on how they are used. Klink and Lockett compare five different types of biblical theology: descriptive history, redemptive history, metanarrative (worldview-story), a canonical view

Strategic storytelling rests on the assumption that the biblical story is a metanarrative (a rival worldview story). However, within this overarching story is the fundamental structure of salvation history.

1.6 The key to grasping the meaning of the biblical story is presenting it as a metanarrative.

So, as a metanarrative, the biblical story has a beginning, middle, and end. It has intention. The protagonist is God Himself. It is not man on center stage discovering a god, creating a sense of being, and establishing meaning.[13] God is the great initiator, revealing Himself to the peoples of the world over time as Sovereign Creator and Redeemer.

It is here we depart from Thomas Boomershine, who writes, "The freedom of the listener to respond in a variety of ways is built into the stories (of the Bible). They do not have only one meaning but open out onto a broad playground of meaning. There, the listeners are invited to play".[14] We would agree that there may be multiple meanings in a story, but meaning is not up for grabs. Rather, meaning is contained within the parameters of the authors' literary piece(s).

2. RELATED TO THE HOLY SPIRIT

2.1 The Holy Spirit engifts and enables.

The Spirit of God empowers the storyteller and enables the story hearer (John 14:25–26; 16:13; 1 Corinthians 2:4, 10, 12–13; 1 John 2:27; also cp. 2 Timothy 2:15). What does this mean? What does this not mean?

In ancient Hebrew the verb stems for "teach" and "learn" are the same.

> "Now, Israel, hear the decrees and laws I am about to teach you.
> Follow them so that you may live and may go in and take possession of the land the Lord, the God of your ancestors, is giving you"
> (Deuteronomy 4:1, NIV).

---

of Scripture, and theological history (Klink and Lockett, *Understanding Biblical Theology*).

13. Buber, *The Eclipse of God*.

14. Boomershine, *Story Journey*, 52.

"Moses summoned all Israel and said: Hear, Israel, the decrees and laws I declare in your hearing today. Learn them and be sure to follow them" (Deuteronomy 5:1, NIV).

To teach is to cause to learn. Learning is not simply acquiring knowledge. Learning in the biblical sense involves changing. What I used to say and do, I no longer say and do. In his epistles, The Apostle Paul says, "to put off the old nature" with its deceitful desires and corrupt manner of life (Ephesians 4:22–24). What I never said and did before, and may not have known to say and do, I now say and do. Again, Paul says, "to put on the new nature" created in true righteousness and holiness. This level of changing or learning is miraculous and is indeed a work of the Holy Spirit.

2.2 Together with the Holy Spirit, God uses human affordance and agency.

To what degree and in what capacities does the Holy Spirit empower? Interestingly, human affordance and agency are employed. The Deuteronomy text says Moses taught. Second Timothy 2:15 is clear that the learner studies or, more accurately, works hard. In this regard the Bible makes no distinction between those who are and are not followers of God. That is, that one simply needs to hear a story but the other needs to be taught. Both need teaching/learning. This is clear in Paul's ministry in the Book of Acts, when he taught in the synagogues, disputing and persuading others for months about the Kingdom of God.

As a follower of Christ who desires to share the Gospel of the Lord Jesus Christ with Catalan speakers in Barcelona, Spain, will I be granted the capacity to proficiently speak Catalan without previously studying the language? No. To what degree does he enable the story hearer? In Barcelona, if I were to share the Gospel in English, would a Catalan hearer understand me apart from having previously acquired some level of English proficiency? No.

If the Holy Spirit has generally not enabled speakers to communicate apart from language acquisition, what about culture and its acquisition? Linguist and translation theorist Eugene Nida argued that culture and language are inseparable.[15] If I tell a story in the language of the host society, but the story characters, norms, plot, and setting are not familiar culturally

---

15. Nida, *Customs and Cultures*, 213.

to the host society, does the Holy Spirit intervene and enable the hearer to understand the foreign story anyway? Rarely, if ever.

Strategic storytelling assumes the Holy Spirit works in the hearts of hearers to prepare them for the message of the Bible. The Synoptic Gospels record a parable Jesus told about four types of soil. Later Jesus explained that the types of soil represent the degree of receptivity to the message or seed that is sown.

However, the authors of this work do not assume that the Holy Spirit normally bypasses the phenomena of language and culture that God Himself created. The sender in communication must utilize a medium of communication that is familiar to the receiver in order to impart a message. Only thereby will the receiver accurately decode the message that is encoded by the sender. This most basic element of communication theory, originating in academic literature with Claude Shannon and Warren Weaver, is artfully described in 1 Corinthians 14:1–11 (ESV):

> "1Pursue love, and earnestly desire the spiritual gifts, especially that you may prophesy. 2For one who speaks in a tongue speaks not to men but to God; for no one understands him, but he utters mysteries in the Spirit. 3On the other hand, the one who prophesies speaks to people for their upbuilding and encouragement and consolation. 4The one who speaks in a tongue builds up himself, but the one who prophesies builds up the church. 5Now I want you all to speak in tongues, but even more to prophesy. The one who prophesies is greater than the one who speaks in tongues, unless someone interprets, so that the church may be built up. 6Now, brothers, if I come to you speaking in tongues, how will I benefit you unless I bring you some revelation or knowledge or prophecy or teaching? 7If even lifeless instruments, such as the flute or the harp, do not give distinct notes, *how will anyone know* what is played? 8And if the bugle gives an indistinct sound, who will get ready for battle? 9So with yourselves, if with your tongue you utter speech that is not intelligible, *how will anyone know* what is said? For you will be speaking into the air. 10There are doubtless many different languages in the world, and none is without meaning, 11but *if I do not know the meaning of the language, I will be a foreigner to the speaker and the speaker a foreigner to me.*" (emphasis added)

2.3 The Holy Spirit does not always "clean up" the mess.

Is not it instructive to note that Paul's text in 1 Corinthians 14 does not suggest that the Holy Spirit supernaturally intervenes when the languages of the sender and receiver differ? The Holy Spirit does not make clear the cultural meaning associated with previously unknown symbols. The meaning of the bugle sound after it has been sounded is not mystically or miraculously converted into that of, say, a cello. It remains a bugle sound.

In September 1996, Tom Steffen presented a paper at the Evangelical Missiological Society in Orlando, Florida, entitled "Flawed Evangelism: The Holy Spirit as Clean-up Hitter" (see Steffen, 1998). Of course, his analogy is from baseball, where the "cleanup" hitter bats fourth in the lineup, traditionally, the batter with the most power. His task is to "clean up the bases" if batters ahead of him got on base but were unable to score a run. The cleanup hitter is expected to deliver big hits in important situations. By way of application, Steffen argues, among other things, that a flawed evangelism approach, such as an over emphasis on urgency, should not falsely assume the Holy Spirit will intervene with inexplicable effectiveness.

3. ASSUMPTIONS RELATED TO TIME

3.1 Efficiency and effectiveness are inextricably connected.

As in all of human life, there is tension in ministry between effectiveness and efficiency. Effectiveness requires time. Efficiency tends to reduce time. Many cross-cultural workers choose efficiency and therefore expediency. For example, when asked, "How much do American Western values, such as expediency and pragmatism, drive CPMs (church planting movements)?" David Garrison responded this way: "The highly indigenous nature of CPMs renders this a non-issue".[16] This pragmatic response does not address the cultural factors in indigenous areas that explain why locals rapidly adopt Western approaches.

On one occasion after traveling into the region of Samaria, Jesus told his disciples, "Don't you have a saying, 'It's still four months until harvest'? I tell you, open your eyes and look at the fields! They are ripe for harvest" (John 4:35). He seems to speak of urgency.

---

16. Schattner, *The Wheel Model*, 112.

Historic dispensational theology argues for an imminent return of the Lord Jesus Christ. This theme among others justifies the urgency of evangelism.[17] Some go further. In September 2010, Bryant Wright, President of the Southern Baptist Convention, said, "Because we're to preach the Gospel of the Kingdom to every ethnos, every people group . . . and then Jesus says He will come. Now folks, listen, are you listening? He ain't comin' until we take the Gospel to every ethnos." So, there is urgency to evangelism based on eschatology (see 2 Peter 3:12).

However, in what ways would urgency impact effectiveness? "Slow is the new fast" is a recent business mantra. It assumes that the best and fastest way to get effectiveness, quality, and sustainability is to slow down. In what ways is God in a hurry? Should we introduce "hurried" as one of His relative attributes?

3.2 Urgency may be the enemy of necessity.

Which of the following needs in the hearers within a host society can be met hurriedly?

1. To unlearn a worldview with all its core presuppositions about reality

2. To let go of emotionally embraced value-dimensions

3. To loosen trust in family and community leaders who, for all one's life, have espoused a particular worldview

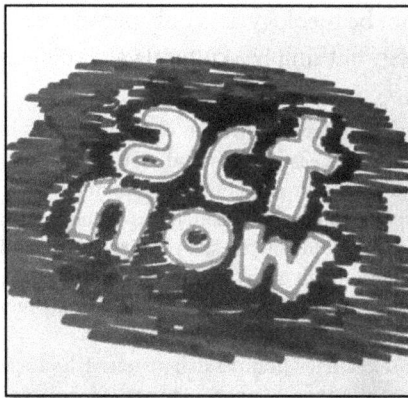

Figure 9.2: Urgency . . . Enemy

17. See May 2013 issue of SBC Life: Journal of the Southern Baptist Convention.

4. To gain trust in a new storyteller who is an outsider without history in our community

5. To comprehend the big picture story of the Bible with its clusters of controlling symbols and stories

6. To put confidence in this new story

7. To embrace a new worldview with its core assumptions about reality, its value-dimensions, and all their impact on our socio-cultural institutions

8. To realize that the new way of life may be one of suffering rather than lavish material riches currently enjoyed by the West

9. To recognize that my new identity is "in Christ" alone and not the high status of the storyteller from the West

10. To stop saying and doing what was common to the old order of things

Strategic storytelling agrees that there is urgency to evangelism and discipleship. However, none of the items listed above is hurry-able. Each takes time. Dependability and sustainability require time. Colossians 3:23–24 says, "Whatever you do, work heartily, as for the Lord and not for men, knowing that from the Lord you will receive the inheritance as your reward. You are serving the Lord Christ".

The haste, speed, brevity, and "bottom-line-up-front" (BLUF) are all part of the package of pragmatism and expediency that so dominates Western culture. We would go further than Ted Ward by adding that the starting point actually may not be theology. It is only perceived as theology. In point of fact it is not theology but simply a cultural value-dimension of the West.[18]

---

18. Dr. Jill Derby began by saying that she wanted to tell the story of the Kurdish fighters stopping ISIL at Erbil, the largest city and capital of Kurdistan. She paused as we finished our lunch in the West Ballroom at the Broadmoor Hotel. The Colorado Springs World Affairs Council sponsored the luncheon. It was September 9, 2014. She continued, "I would be remiss if I simply told you the story of Erbil. You would not understand it. The only way you can understand it is if you hear the whole story. So, I want to start with World War I and tell you what has happened over the last one hundred years. In 1918, the British and French divided . . . "

Dr. Derby took one hour and ten minutes to lay a foundation across time. She was not hurried. She put the story bits, themes, anchor stories, symbols, and characters together to form a big picture. Finally, at the end, when she did explain what happened in Erbil, it all made sense. We knew why the Kurdish *peshmerga* was emboldened. We knew why President Obama drew a line at Erbil but not at Kirkuk, even though US soldiers had bitterly fought for Kirkuk.

4. RELATED TO THE STORYTELLER

4.1 A storyteller must attain and maintain credibility.

Not only must the story come across with fidelity and coherence, so must the storyteller.[19] A storyteller tells symbol-based stories. Story hearers may or may not be familiar with him. The same may be true of his stories. In a world of credulity, a lack of familiarity is not an issue. But, ours is not a world of credulity. Rival storytellers, narratives, and symbols are everywhere. And not all of them are true. Truly it is a world of incredulity and, given the dispensation of things, well it should be. We must ask first and foremost, "Who is the storyteller?" Then, and only then, we should also ask, "What is the credibility of the story?"

In his book *God as Storyteller*, Old Testament scholar John Beck analyzes the Bible from the perspective of the storyteller, God Himself.[20] How does he introduce himself? How does he imbue stories with meaning? On what basis does he make meaning? When the story is told, what do we think of him and what has he left with us?[21]

She used stories, character descriptions, and maps. Here and there she inserted personal reflections.

I saw all four types of rhetorical discourse. She *narrated* the story. Intermittently, as necessary, she inserted *exposition*, making sure the details of the plot were clear. Often she *described* aspects of the culture that she knew we would not understand. And, she powerfully *argued* for Kurdistan independence by emphasizing four recurring themes.

19. Fisher, *Human Communication as Narration*.

20. Beck, *God as Storyteller*.

21. My paternal grandfather, a member of the Augusta Country Club in Augusta, Georgia, introduced me to golf, shared "hand-me-down" equipment and supplies, and had me accompany him to the Club for rounds of golf, meals, and introductions to his friends. Stories accompanied everything. I learned that the Club was geographically adjacent to the August National Golf Club, the home of the Masters Golf Tournament. I learned now to play golf. And, I learned the etiquette of golf, which transcended the fairways and greens. At lunch we learned how to conduct ourselves in that social setting. It was the ideal place to meet prominent attorneys and newspaper editors in the city. My grandfather, the Vice-President of the Georgia Power Company, was a Republican, President of the Augusta Chamber of Commerce, and known everywhere in the city. When Papa recommended to me to use a seven-iron on my approach to the 18th green, I trusted him. And, I believed the things he told me about politics.

On the other hand, my maternal grandfather lived on rented property outside of Antreville, South Carolina. He was a cotton farmer in Abbeville County. He hired Black families to pick the cotton, which he hauled to the gin on a wagon pulled by horses. Grandpa did not read or write. Our family frequently visited him. We used the outhouse, drew water from the well, hunted, and learned how to play a local form of checkers called "pool". Pool

Does not it seem arrogant for a storyteller to assume he can enter a society from the outside and, as a stranger, tell a believable rival story? The arrogance is in the assumption that he and his story will have credibility. But, in fact, neither will, without the establishment of trust bonds across time and amidst authentic relationships.[2223]

The quest for the storyteller is not simply to replace symbols and tell stories but also to acquire trust. Jesus' earthly ministry may a good model to follow. Consider the factors that were involved in his quest to establish his believability and authority. He humbled himself and became a man. He lived among people. He endured human limitations. He grew up in a household of a family in a community. He worked. He served others at the most basic level of human need (the sick, hungry, and isolated). He tended to women and children. He studied Scripture and taught with authority. What the Scripture said, he lived. Modeling is essential for meaning transfer. It demonstrates in real life the authenticity of stated truths. Jim Lo is correct when he states that "It would be hard to be influenced by strangers."[24]

---

checkers may have originated in the 1930s and was played predominantly by Blacks.

Grandpa also told me stories . . . how to plant and harvest upland cotton, drawing water from the well without stirring up dirt in the well bottom, controlling odor in the outhouse, his relationships with the Black families who worked for him, and the importance of U.S. government subsidies for the success of cotton farmers. Of course, he was a Democrat. When Grandpa recommended to me that we fish when the moon was full and early in the morning, I trusted him. And, I believed the things he told me about politics.

To this day I find it easy to leverage divergent political views. I see how taxes hurt and help at the same time. I still play golf and some of my better friends are Black Americans.

22. Meyers, *Christianity Confronts Culture*, 5.

23. Abraham Maslow has provided an inimitable model. One must start with involvement in basic human needs, at the bottom, and from there attain and maintain believability on a quest to one day earn the right to share stories at the top of the pyramid of human needs. Maslow writes, "What a man can be, he must be" (Maslow, *A Theory of Human Motivation*, 91). Existing stories in a society already inform self-actualization. Grandparents and others have already told stories about what is and is not . . . about what ought and ought not to be.

24. Guthrie, *Missions in the Third Millennium*, 88.

5. RELATED TO THE METHODOLOGY OF STORY

5.1 What a story does not do.

According to basic communication theory[25], a sender and receiver en-code and decode messages that are exchanged through a medium. The story medium alone, or in other words the story structure (plot, characters, and setting), does not guarantee that encoding and decoding will match. Communication, from *communis*, is the means whereby meaning "is made common". The degree to which commonness does not exist is the degree to which communication will not take place.

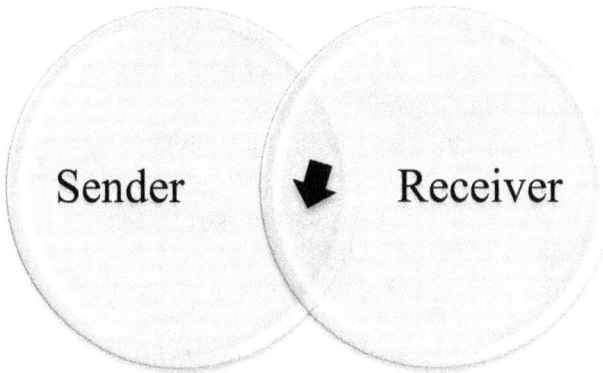

Figure 9.3: Common Language, Culture, Structures, Value-Dimensions, and Worldview Core Presuppositions

5.2 TELLING A NEW STORY DOES NOT MECHANICALLY DISPLACE EXISTING SYMBOLS AND STORIES.

Closely related to communication theory above, the telling of a story does not automatically displace existing symbols and stories in the host society. Adding a story to the overall set of stories does not reduce the total number of existing stories in a "zero-sum" game. Adding rival symbols and stories to existing ones increases the total numbers. It is this environment that

---

25. See Claude E. Shannon and Warren Weaver in *A Mathematical Theory of Communication*, 1948, for a venerable, ground-breaking model of human communication.

supports syncretism, allows legalism, and nurtures nominalism. None of these is helpful. They are damaging to everyone in a community. The measure of effective communication must go beyond what a hearer begins doing (for example, obeying Christ's commands). It must also evaluate what a hearer stops doing or "puts off". Even further, it must assess motivation. Why are they obeying Christ's commands?

5.3 Worldview displacement is not easy.

Worldview core presuppositions are not easily displaced or altered by symbol and story. New symbols and stories are always interpreted on the basis of existing worldview core presuppositions in the host society. The principle problem globally is that the hearer who decodes the story is a prisoner of his own cultural norms. Human agency is needed to help deconstruct old presuppositions and construct new ones.

Telling the big picture story of the Bible, story sets, or isolated biblical stories does not make up for what the storyteller does not understand about the existing worldview in the host society. Worldview classifications are derived from anchor symbols informed by controlling narratives. These controlling narratives are trusted more than new rival symbols and stories from the Bible.

6. RELATED TO LANGUAGE, CULTURE, AND WORLDVIEW

6.1 Culture is deeply embedded.

Culture is the learned, shared patterns of perception and behavior. No one is born with cultural perceptions. They are learned across time, in varied circumstances, and generally in the midst of endeared relationships. They are shared in community through symbol-based stories reinforced through ritual. Although each of us has peculiarities, almost all of what we say and do is also said and done by others around us. Just as people in South Carolina speak differently from people in Southern California, so it is in Argentina, where Castellano in Cordoba differs from Castellano in Buenos Aires. Similarly, the gait of a German walk is common to most Germans but differs from that of Tamils in the south of India.

Cultural perceptions in the mind and heart of people are deeply embedded. Social scientists describe them as core worldview assumptions and emotionally embraced value-dimensions. Most students of culture know of organizational anthropologist Geert Hofstede's research related to value-dimensions. These "ought's" and "ought not's" are powerful drivers that are below the surface of observable culture. Fewer students are familiar with anthropologist Michael Kearney from the University of California Riverside. Kearney's research identifies six classifications of core worldview presuppositions. He posits that a worldview is made up of perceptions related to self, other, relationships, causality, time, and space.[26]

Through the research of anthropologist Edward T. Hall, we know that both value-dimensions and core worldview presuppositions are generally outside of the awareness of most people. They are tacitly assumed. Although invisible from the surface, value-dimensions and core worldview presuppositions are powerful forces. They are like wind, gravity, nuclear energy, or electricity. The untrained eye does not generally see these forces in the natural world. But there is no escaping their impact.

In fact, so powerful is culture that Sherwood Lingenfelter, student of George Murdock at the University of Pittsburgh, argues that culture is a virtual "prison of disobedience".[27] What we eat, think tastes good, how we dress, whom we consider friends, our likes, morals, and so much more are all defined and shaped by culture. It seems perpetual. Can culture change? Yes. But cultural change is generally slow and deliberate.[28]

6.2 Culture trumps story.

The influence of an existing culture outmaneuvers the power of a new story. This is true frequently if not always. Said more explicitly, the existing symbols and stories in a society are more influential than new ones. Why? Existing symbols and stories have already been handed down from relatives and local leaders who are trusted across time. An outsider introduces the new symbols and stories into a society. To what degree has the outsider established authentic relationships and trust bonds with local people? In such a context, the power of culture trumps the power of rival symbols and

26. Kearney, *World View*.

27. Lingenfelter, *Transforming Culture*, 19–22, 123.

28. It is understood that some facets of culture may be altered rapidly through natural disasters, wars, or other catastrophic events.

stories. In *The Theft of History*, social anthropologist Jack Goody writes, "I necessarily see the world through my own eyes, not with those of another".[29]

6.3 Flawed methods put meaning in jeopardy.

Given these established truths about language, culture, and worldview, simply telling a brief Bible story with the hope that God will mystically or miraculously intervene is to put at jeopardy the very meaning of that biblical story. In fact, to do so is fundamentally disrespectful of the Bible and impertinent to the men, women, and children who so desperately need to understand its meaning. Cross-cultural storytellers rarely grasp the detrimental power of culture in distorting the biblical message. We wish the Holy Spirit would intervene and hit a homerun in every game, clearing the bases. Unfortunately, this is not his modus operandi.

CONCLUDING REFLECTIONS

"*Beware of shortcuts!*" *Strategic storytelling* assumes that culture trumps rival symbols and stories. That is, the power of existing symbols and stories—which are diachronic, locally derived, and told by known, reliable people—are more powerful than new rival symbols and stories, which may seem synchronic, are not local, and have been introduced by unknown outsiders.

Theologically, the authors do not believe that the Scripture itself or the Holy Spirit mystically or miraculously dissolve the existing stories (also known by the term *culture*), solve the problem of time and locality, and absolve naturally occurring mistrust toward the outsider storyteller. The new symbols and stories remain an undefined bugle sound. Prayerfully and assiduously following the processes outlined in the twelve-step methodology can help bring clear meaning to the bugle sound.

29. Goody, *The Theft of History*, 13.

10

Anticipating the Future

DO NOT JUST FOLLOW FADS

RECENTLY, ON BEHALF OF Worldview Resource Group (WRG), I visited a well-known foundation to propose a ministry project. Soon into the presentation, the foundation's Executive Director redirected our conversation from metrics to methodology. He asked if WRG had ever heard of storytelling. He shared that it had emerged in the providence of God as the latest and best practice in global missions. He called it a "breakthrough" technique. I was unable to explain that the "Father of Storytelling in Missions" sat on the WRG Board. My feeble attempt to implant storytelling into a more complete methodology was unimpressive. Hmm . . . I wondered if storytelling were being viewed as a fad.

A *fad* is any behavior that is collectively and enthusiastically followed for a brief period of time. When I was in high school the boys wore crushed velour flared-leg pants with platform shoes. It was the 70s. I may be somewhat embarrassed to do so today.

But just because something is a fad does not mean it is not beneficial. My wife and I have eaten a Paleo diet for several years. It works. We both have returned to the weight we enjoyed when we were in our thirties. Our health is excellent.

However, we did not just abruptly launch into a menu of fish, sweet potatoes, nuts, and carrots. First, we researched what the Paleo menu was and was not. We read and listened to others. Both of us consulted our physicians and had blood work done to establish a base line. Healthcare professionals supported our decision to transition to the menu. Along the way we continue to be monitored by our physicians.

Storytelling has been both a fad and an effective method of communication. On the fad side, as WRG consultants minister globally, they encounter people who have "become" storytellers. They had heard about storytelling and decided to do it. So, rather than teaching topically across cultures, they now tell stories from the Bible. Sometimes it is any story out of the Bible. Almost always the storytelling is on autopilot. It is not contextualized into locally familiar cultural functions and forms. The cross-cultural workers tell stories the way they have always told stories. Looking ahead, this is the topic of book four in the series, "There is More to the Story". How should we adapt our style of storytelling across cultures?

In these cases, storytelling is more faddish than strategic. Tellers have not done research. They have not consulted experts. They do not necessarily know where storytelling fits into a larger more holistic approach to ministry or how to do it across cultures. At times, in quiet moments, a number of cross-cultural workers have shared with WRG consultants that storytelling actually does not work.

We have argued in this book that storytelling itself is not the problem. The problem lies in the larger approach.

DO ASK QUESTIONS

If we were praying and planning to minister in Morocco, what would be key questions to ask? Here are a few:

1. What method have you employed, unwittingly, simply because it is a fad?

2. What are your actual methods of ministry across culture? List them on a piece of paper. Is there a developmental flow to them? All together, what are they as a whole?

3. Why are you doing what you are doing? Analyze what you do. If you feel the Holy Spirit just leads you to do something, what biblical principles support that leading? What missiological foundations undergird how you do what you do? Have your methods been proven over time? Have others used them and experienced effectiveness? Would you not agree that the answers to these questions would affirm whether or not the Holy Spirit is actually leading you?

4. What metrics are available to assess your effectiveness? Currently, I am providing cultural competency training to a large United States Government agency. Participants work along the Southwest border of the United States and Mexico. The training was designed with stated broad goals and specific objectives. Metrics have been established to evaluate effectiveness. In what way is the dial being moved? If this is a valid aspect of training and communicating in the public sector, why would it not also be equally valid for the biblical storyteller?

5. Is the data you are using to measure your success valid and reliable?

6. Of the twelve steps in the methodology presented in this book, which ones have you already put into practice? Do not forget the acuity of each step. So, to what degree have you implemented a step?

7. Which ones are missing in your approach to cross-cultural ministry? Why are they missing? Are you able to identify the assumptions underlying what you are doing and what you are not doing?

8. What is a mentor saying about what you do and how you do it? For several years I met with Hugh Eaton, the Co-Founder of the Weather Channel, twice a month. Hugh's experience was inimitable. He was a member of the First Presbyterian Church in Colorado Springs, Colorado, and a faithful disciple of the Lord Jesus Christ. We talked endlessly about Worldview Resource Group, and I will always be grateful for his insights.

9. If you were able to develop trusted friendships with locals in a cross-cultural context, what are they saying to you about your activity and impact? I now hear candid comments from Dr. Jayakumar Ramachandran in Bangalore, India. We have worked together in India for a decade.

10. To what degree are you really open to reconsider your approach, its underlying assumptions, and its success? Hugh Eaton used to say, "Some people, if they do not know it already, you are not going to tell them".

In other words, evaluate what you are doing and why.

DO CONSIDER THESE PARADIGM SHIFTS

In book one of the series, Steffen highlights the paradigm shifts that have already taken place in the Orality Movement. His insights are based on a lifetime of work in the field and on his reflections related to storytelling.

Steffen was among the very first cross-cultural workers to incorporate storytelling into a ministry methodology. He and others planted reproducing churches among the Ifugao people in Luzon, Philippines.

In this book I now appeal for five additional shifts in thinking and approaching cross-cultural ministry.[1] Here they are . . . anticipating the future:

1. Paradigm Shift One—About the Bible

In humility we ought to repent for using Scripture as an animistic juju. Its physical properties possess no magical powers. There is nothing unique about the cover, paper, binding, edging, marker ribbon, or ink. Irrespective of the language in which it was written, the mere recitation of its words yields no effectual consequence.[2]

Rather, in faith we must trust the content of Scripture, that is, its salvation history story. It is the truth of Scripture that is powerful. And, it is through understanding and responding to the truth, effectively communicated, whereby change takes place in a hearer's life. So, going forward, our earnest effort in dependence upon the Holy Spirit is to effectively communicate the content of Scripture to maximize the hearer's understanding and response. The objective is not simply telling a story. We ought to tell to teach ($t2T$).

2. Paradigm Shift Two—About the Holy Spirit

Based upon the clarity of Scripture, we ought to trust in the powerful work of the Holy Spirit but not confuse his efficacy with a kind of evangelical

---

1. Five Additional Paradigms:
    1. About the Bible
    2. About the Holy Spirit
    3. About Story
    4. About Teaching
    5. About Time and Relationships

2. Here we differ markedly from Islam. The recitation of the Qur'an must be done properly and by the right person. The recitation itself brings blessing. Arabic consonants and vowels must be pronounced precisely with all their melodic beauty (thickness, thinness, pharyngealization, prolongation, and more). In fact, *tajweed* refers to the rules governing the pronunciation during the recitation of the Qur'an. One such reciter, a renowned *qari*, is Abdul Al Sudais. With a PhD in Islamic studies, he is the leading imam of the Grand Mosque in Mecca. His recitation is famous for voice and emotion.

sorcery. His power to intervene does not supplant my responsibility to implement insights reflected in the twelve steps.

3. Paradigm Shift Three—About Story

While story indeed is a powerful medium of communication, it is no panacea. Simply converting salvation history topics to a narrative format is not the totality of an effective cross-cultural ministry strategy. As we anticipate ministry in the future, we ought to use story but embed it in a valid and reliable holistic methodology. We should stop confusing the part for the whole. In this book we have attempted to present that whole.

4. Paradigm Shift Four—About Teaching

One common narrative, a false one, says teaching is in opposition to storytelling. Some people assume, inaccurately, that this is a new, previously unattained, insight. Teaching is actually an integral part of storytelling. Teaching facilitates knowledge, description, application, analysis, synthesis, and evaluation.

A fatal flaw in the storytelling approach of the global mission enterprise is the assumption that merely hearing or experiencing a story results in learning. Not necessarily. John Dewey writes, "We do not learn from experience . . . we learn from reflecting on experience".[34] I have had the privilege to "teach" at many levels. Recently, the largest service nonprofit in Canada hired me as a consultant to help them with a horizontal merger with another prominent service nonprofit. In another setting I have had the delight of walking alongside a co-worker as she applied and was accepted into an exclusive PhD program of strategic communication at Arizona State University (ASU). At the collegiate level, I have the opportunity to facilitate courses in intercultural communication and social research design. And, I have had the indescribable joy of helping my grandson set up a post-war Lionel O-27 electric train.

In every situation, stories alone would have failed. In Canada, my stories of past feasibility studies, corporate consolidations, and mergers have laid a

3. Dewey, *How We Think*, 78.

4. It is said that this is a spurious quote from John Dewey. It is attributed to *How we think* published in 1933. If it is not a direct quote from Dewey, the aphorism is an accurate reflection of his emphases.

foundation. But alone they were not enough. I also helped my clients understand, through careful explanation, what to do in their unique situation.

My personal stories of applying and being accepted to Biola University's School of Intercultural Studies enabled me to connect more closely with my coworker. But, she still needed to adapt my insights to ASU.

My acquired knowledge of the Lionel tradition, locomotives, tenders, track gauge, switches, and low voltage transformers was one thing. It was an altogether different thing to walk step-by-step through the assembly and usage of the set with someone I loved. "Insert the pins here in the track and tighten the connection like this . . . " "Yes! Just like that!" "Good work!" "See . . . it is this middle track that will complete the electronic connection." At every level, storytelling and teaching occurred side by side.

5. Paradigm Shift Five—About Time and Relationships

Yes, there is no substitute for an endearing relationship. They are built over time and in varied circumstances. We can be blind to our own cultural influences related to time and relationships. Blindness causes missteps. Kathy Trickey, with whom I have worked training veterinarians on the Mexican border who inspect imported livestock, says, "In our training programs we 'unhide' culture to its own participants".

Generally, the West is abrupt and blunt. We expect quick results. Many in the world see our personal relationships as shallow. As we anticipate the future, we need to slow down. We must take whatever time is needed to build authentic relationships with people. Effective ministry is costly—yet how rewarding.

CONCLUDING REFLECTIONS

Just as Jesus needed to explain his comments to the disciples in Mark 13, so it is with us in our ministries across cultures. There is more to the story. We do not simply tell stories; we tell to teach . . . t2T. We can increase our effectiveness if we use storytelling in the broader context of mindful engagement.[5] The twelve steps of strategic storytelling provide insights for effective engagement.

5. See the Edwards-Strauss-Steiner *Model of Cultural Context Awareness of Self and Others* in the Appendices.

Appendix A

Essential Steps of Field Research

1. Pre-entry research
2. Choose a geographic location in a host society; note the following issues:
   - Physical acclimation (climate, lodging, diet, and lifestyle procedures)
   - Regional permissions and sponsorship for "transfer of trust"
   - Respect for local norms
   - Residency and migration patterns of local population
3. Establish relationships
4. Cultural adjustment:
   a. Self-awareness of one's own culture helps the cross-cultural worker understand personal expectations
   b. "Deprivation of norm" generally results in an inability to predict what may happen and insecurity amidst strangeness
   c. Manage the adjustment process by practicing the four D's:
      - *Delay* major decisions. Why? Time will remedy upheaval.
      - *Divulge* to a colleague that there is a struggle. Why? The need is for me to adjust rather than conclude "they" are stupid.
      - *Develop* a relationship with a local counterpart. Why? To "see" the stranger as a person.

- *Delight* in one's identity (that is, drink a Coke or enjoy a *futbol* match). Why? Adjusting to another culture is not abandoning one's own identity.

5. Initial language familiarity and acquisition (the degree of culture and language acquisition is determined by two basic factors: how well do participants speak a common language and what is the task to be done)

6. General surveying and mapping: physical layout, avenues of migration, nodes (crossing and convergence), features, ownership, population, names/titles, kinship, means and production, material culture, observable behavior, events, community structure (social and political), symbols, rituals, socio-cultural institutions, status, roles, gestures, gaits, art/play, and practical expressions.

7. Typically, empirical research involves the data collection techniques of *observing* and *interviewing* (usually in that order)

8. Observation may take several forms: indirect, direct, and participant

9. What to observe depends on the purpose of the research. All research across cultures is regulated by Grounded Theory, that is, that conclusions are derived from or grounded in research data. Most research is initiated with questions and hypotheses.

10. The Outline of Cultural Materials informs potential categories of observation.[1]

11. All researchers rely on precedent literature to form a framework of theoretical constructs.

12. Interviewing also is done in different ways depending on its purpose: unstructured, semi-structured, and structured.

13. Direct questions, a common style in low context Western culture, are not effective in cross-cultural research. The reason is obvious, that is, they contain the biased categories of the researcher. Story-solicitation is far more productive.

14. Cultural data obtained through data collection techniques (whether images, video, or audio recordings) is described in writing on a template for field notes and organized in folders (written and/or

---

1. See http://hraf.yale.edu

electronic). Research software such as *NVivo* 10 is available to help researchers organize and analyze field data.

15. How many observations and interviews are required to justify a conclusion? Statistical research shows that for a data population of less than 1,000, a random sample of 30 percent must be surveyed. In other words, the researcher must observe 300 cultural events or interview 300 culture helpers. For populations up to 5,000, 10 percent is sufficient for generalizations.

16. Four tools for data analysis include:

   a. Successive approximation

   b. Coding—open, axial, and selective, with items, units, categories, structures, and systems based on local phenomenological perspective (emic versus etic)

   c. The model of culture developed by Worldview Resource Group and adapted by Global Perspectives Consulting provides a pathway from observable behavior toward understanding shared values and core worldview assumptions.

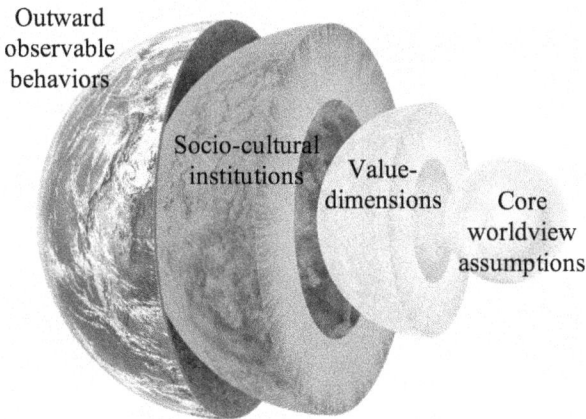

Outward observable behaviors

Socio-cultural institutions

Value-dimensions

Core worldview assumptions

Figure A.1: Model of Culture

   d. Story analysis: noting repetitive themes, metaphors, and transitions

17. Results are written and published in a format that introduces the research, reviews related literature, describes the research methodology, and offers generalizations grounded in research data.

The degree of cultural differences from local region to local region is greatly underestimated by outsiders. For example, within the metropolis of Bangalore (Bengaluru), India there are numerous districts. Walking from the city district of Horamavu across the Horamavu Overpass into the city district of Banaswadi, one would cross the Outer Ring Road. The walk would be less than one kilometer. Both districts are on the northeast side of the city.

The trade language of Bangalore and the entire state of Karnataka is Kannada. One would also hear other languages including Hindi and English. In some neighborhoods of Banaswadi, Tamil is the dominant language. It is entirely possible that Kannada, Hindi, English, and Tamil speakers would not understand each other. The origin of the Tamil speakers is Tamil Nadu, from the south. Hindi is the dominant language in the northwest of India. Most educated people would speak English, but with a strong accent influenced by their mother tongue, say Kannada or Tamil.

Appendix B

Four Overarching Patterns of Culture

DIVERSE RESPONSES FROM DIFFERENT people in cross-cultural settings reflect different overarching patterns of culture. I may respond truthfully to an inquiry. I was raised up in a culture that is justice-oriented. We speak the truth and do so as clearly as we can. But a counterpart in a cross-cultural setting may answer the same inquiry in such a way that "face" is maintained by all present. Reputations are protected. In such a case, the counterpart would have been raised up in a culture that is honor-oriented. They bestow honor upon whom it has been ascribed.

This description compares and contrasts four overarching patterns of culture. It attempts to impart understanding. It provides the language needed. These four are not the only patterns of cultures, but these do dominant people's behavior around the world and are interesting to consider. The comparison and contrast will rework topics that may be familiar to some. Each of the four individual patterns is (re)titled per its defining feature.

A "pattern" is something that is deliberately repeated and thereby is predictable. That something could be a mechanical design, a musical arrangement, an artistic work, a personal preference, or a natural configuration. A pattern is generally intelligible. That is, with adequate knowledge, an observer gets the intended form and may even comprehend its function and meaning.

The adjective "overarching" signifies influencing or dominating. Either meaning applies to these patterns. My orientation toward justice influences everything I think, say, and do. An equal characterization can be made about an orientation toward honor. In *Patterns of Culture* (1934), Ruth Benedict uses the expression, " . . . great arc(s) of potential human behaviour".[1] A pattern of culture is overarching if a preponderance of people lives it out, feels deeply about it, can clearly articulate its place in society, and ties it to one's own story (history, identity, and trajectory).

This explanation sees four overarching patterns of culture: justice, honor, clientelism, and harmony. These differentiations are not modern. The societal advantages and disadvantages of guilt and shame are mentioned in the *Analects of Confucius*, a work that may be as old as 500 BCE. In the early twentieth century, sociologist Max Weber analyzes the role of guilt in Protestantism and its impact on western capitalism.[2] In 1946, anthropologist Ruth Benedict describes the role of honor and shame in Japanese culture in her well-known work, *Chrysanthemum and the Sword*.[3] Later in 1954, as an introduction to the discipline of missiology, linguist Eugene Nida mentions three orientations of culture: fear, shame, and guilt.[4] A follower of Emile Durkheim, British anthropologist Mary Douglas describes a variation of honor and shame in *Purity and Danger*. Perhaps informed by Nida and now familiar to many, Roland Muller (a pseudonym) compares and contrasts guilt, shame, and fear cultures.[5]

Global Perspectives Consulting inserts a fourth overarching pattern of culture called *clientelism*. Table B.1 unpacks the four patterns following a model of culture where worldview is at the core. Unlike other listings of these differentiations, GPC labels the patterns[6] using a term that best describes the outstanding feature in each. For example, rather than the familiar "guilt/righteousness", GPC uses the term "justice". And, rather than the expression "fear/power", GPC uses the term "harmony".

1. Benedict, *Patterns of Culture*, 219.

2. Weber, *The Protestant Ethic and the Spirit of Capitalism*.

3. Benedict, *Chrysanthemum and the Sword*, 222–227.

4. Nida, *Customs and Cultures*, 150.

5. Muller, *Honor & Shame*.

6. If you are familiar with these differentiations, you recall that some presentations refer to the sets as paradigms or even worldviews. The assessment of GPC is that such designations are mislabels. The terms *paradigm* and *worldview* may be synonyms. GPC calls the sets "overarching patterns of culture", within each of which is a worldview as one component part of the whole.

	Justice	Honor	Clientelism	Harmony
Worldview	Legality	Community	Reciprocity	Security
Value	Righteousness	Reputation	Resources	Respite
Obligation	To written standards	To an honor code	To connections	To holistic interactions
Identity	Guilty or not guilty	Shameful or honorable	Benefited or benefactor	Out of harmony or in harmony
Spotlight	Individual rights	Family name	Relationships	Control
Key Institutions	Codified law, justice system, and law enforcement	Kinship, family, extended family, and integrated community	Exchange, asymmetrical affiliations, and informal networks	The supernatural and natural worlds (not differentiated)
Outward observable behaviors	The truth, individualism, self-efficacy, achieved status, and equality	Conformity, collectivism, "face" per the eyes of others, ascribed status, and hierarchy	Presentation, stratification, and interactions	Community concord, "in" groups, rituals and ceremonies, and religious specialists
Place	The West	The East and Middle East	The South	Global

Table B.1: Four Overarching Patterns of Culture

Justice has been the dominant cultural framework of people in the West for two centuries. Consciously or not, most people in the West have a strong awareness of right versus wrong. Generally, this appreciation of morality is rooted in an obligation to the rule of law. Ultimately in democratic societies, the rule of law rests upon constitutional documents ratified by means of a widely accepted process of development and implementation.

Honor is the dominant cultural framework of almost all people in the East and Middle East. This has been true for millennia. Everyone has an awareness that speech and behavior display respect or disrespect. Although pervasive in all communal relationships, shame and honor are most important amidst the family, extended family, and local community. Note carefully that honor is not necessarily a feeling derived internally as in a justice culture. Honor is an attribution bestowed by others rather than claimed by oneself.

Clientelism is a common cultural framework in the Global South. Throughout life one learns to develop connections with the right people in given circumstances for needed resources. These connections may or may not be characterized as "friendships". The purpose of the connections is not necessarily closeness but reciprocal exchange.

Harmony is prevalent globally in indigenous cultures. The supernatural and natural worlds are not differentiated. All aspects of life are interconnected. Interactions are the key to maintaining harmony in order to be secure.

Any culture may display tendencies from each category but generally one category represents an overarching pattern in a culture.

Appendix C

An Adaptation of the Developmental Model of Intercultural Sensitivity

DENYING THAT CULTURAL DIFFERENCES exist is a more extreme form of ethnocentrism where we assume that our culture is superior. Table C.1 shows the developmental stages of cultural competency from ethnocentrism to ethnorelativism. The term *ethnocentrism* means using one's own culture as the standard for all others. *Ethnorelativism* understands the values and behaviors of others as cultural. From left to right there are six stages of development. At the far left a person denies that cultural differences even exist. At the far right a bilingual person is completely comfortable in two cultures.

An ideal objective for cross-cultural workers is stage four of the developmental model. Stage four is the beginning of ethnorelativism and is identified by the label *Acceptance*. It is important to understand that acceptance is not the same as moral agreement. However, a person who accepts another culture understands some aspects of it and displays appropriate respect.

		Ethnocentric			Ethnorelative		

Denial	Defense	Minimiza-tion	Accep-tance	Adapta-tion	Integra-tion
My cultural experience is the only one that is real and valid. There is little to no thought of "other".	"We" are superior and "they are inferior. One feels threatened and is highly criti-cal. What is strange may be labeled as stupid.	Other cultures are trivialized or roman-ticized. One tends to deny differences (e.g., "color blind") and only seek similarities.	I accept but may not agree with other cultures. Gener-ally, I am curious and respectful.	I "see" the world through differ-ent eyes and make intentional changes in my own behavior and values.	I eas-ily move in and out of different cultural worldviews.

Table C.1: Developmental Model of Intercultural Sensitivity (adapted by Global Perspectives Consulting)

Questions:

1. Do you feel you are more ethnocentric or ethnorelative?

2. If a person were more ethnocentric, how would it impact their at-titudes in a cross-cultural setting?

3. Why does "needs assessment" research often show that cross-cultural workers are more ethnocentric?

4. In what ways would the trait of ethnocentrism impact ministry across cultures?

5. What is one thing a person could do to become more ethnorelative?

Appendix D

The Four Capabilities of Cultural Intelligence (CQ)

CULTURAL INTELLIGENCE (CQ) IS the capability to function effectively across cultures. The Cultural Intelligence Center in Holt, Michigan has identified four sets of capabilities that consistently predict adjustment and performance in intercultural settings. They are CQ Drive, CQ Knowledge, CQ Strategy, and CQ Action.

1. The CQ Drive capability is your natural interest, enjoyment, confidence, and perseverance in cross-cultural situations. To some degree these are intrinsic, deeply rooted in personality, identity, and values. However, CQ Drive may be improved.

What is CQ Drive?	What are its sub-dimensions?	What does high CQ Drive look like?	Personal development tips
A person's motivation to engage others from different backgrounds, behaviors, and worldviews.	• Intrinsic interest • Extrinsic interest • Self-efficacy	High CQ Drive means a willingness to learn and adapt to cultural differences, while low CQ Drive indicates a preference for the familiar.	• Leave the hotel room in Buenos Aires, Argentina and walk about the block • Take the nearby subway to the next stop and back • Go to an adjacent store and buy something you need

Table D.1: CQ Drive

2. CQ Knowledge is your acquired understanding of culture general and specific. How do people behave? What socio-cultural institutions promote and prevent such behavior? What are people's values? Identity markers? What are the core worldview assumptions from which all else is derived? Interestingly, some intercultural training is limited to simply knowledge, without incorporating the remaining 75 percent of CQ capabilities.

What is CQ Knowledge?	What are its sub-dimensions?	What does high CQ Knowledge look like?	Personal development tips
CQ Knowledge refers to your understanding of culture itself and how it works, that is, how it impacts the way people think and behave. CQ Knowledge starts with understanding your own culture.	• Business • Values and norms • Socio-linguistic • Leadership	High CQ Knowledge is displayed by both culture general and culture specific insights.	• Read about the history of the region • Buy and use a Lonely Planet travel guide • Learn ten (10) practical expressions in the local language • Understand a common leadership approach and why

Table D.2: CQ Knowledge

3. CQ Strategy is the extent to which you are aware of yourself and others in an intercultural setting plus your ability to plan how to manage those situations effectively. How does the process of negotiation change in a hierarchical, shame/honor, and high context culture? Applied to cross-cultural ministry, a weighty degree of responsibility in culture adjustment and culture competency lies with the newcomers to any region. They must learn *how* to learn about culture, what questions to ask (internally and to others), what observations to make, what adjustments are necessary, and how to manage personal expectations. The answers are found in CQ Strategy. Planning, awareness, and checking are three integral components of CQ Strategy that are grounded in empirical data from CQ research.

What is CQ Strategy?	What are its sub-dimensions?	What does high CQ Strategy look like?	Personal development tips
CQ Strategy refers to a person's awareness and ability to plan appropriately given cultural dynamics. Going further, CQ Strategy bespeaks of one's ability to understand how to adapt behavior across cultures. Finally, this capability also includes monitoring whether or not a person behaves appropriately in a cross-cultural setting.	• Planning • Awareness • Checking	High CQ Strategy anticipates and predicts cultural events relying on alertness rather than simply moving forward on the basis of semi-automated assumptions and behaviors.	• Do not operate on cruise control • Plan where to go, what to do, and how to relate • Rather than being absorbed in self-consciousness, look up and around at what is happening

Table D.3: CQ Strategy

4. CQ Action is what you actually do in a cross-cultural situation to relate and work. How do you adapt behavior to different cultural norms? To what degree are you able to be flexible?

What is CQ Action?	What are its sub-dimensions?	What does high CQ Action look like?	Personal development tips
CQ Action, refers to the actual behavioral changes a person makes in the cross-cultural setting. It has to do with what we do, whether in Rome, Italy, or at the office in Denver as we work with colleagues who originate from Mumbai, India.	• Speech acts • Verbal • Nonverbal	High CQ Action means a person is comfortable in the cross-cultural context and is able to turn off "auto-pilot" and make adaptations.	• Practice your practical expressions • Make a friend in the host society • Adapt how you speak and behave

Table D.4: CQ Action

The four sets of CQ capabilities are integrated. You may have confidence that you can be effective across cultures, but lack culture general and specific knowledge. In point of fact, you may not be effective. Or, you might have culture knowledge, but not be aware of how to adapt your behavior accordingly. Although CQ drive may be mostly intrinsic, CQ is not a fixed capability. You are able to develop your cross-cultural understanding and skills. A key in this development is reflection. Who are you? What are you doing? Who are others? To what degree are they the same or different?

Appendix E

Etic and Emic Perspectives of Culture

THE TERMS EMIC AND *etic* were coined in 1954 by linguist/anthropologist Kenneth Pike (1912–2000).[1] Pike earned his PhD in linguistics from the University of Michigan, studying under Edward Sapir. Linguistics is the scientific study of human language. For thirty-seven years, Pike was the President of the Summer Institute of Linguistics (known internationally as Wycliffe Bible Translators) based in Norman, Oklahoma. *Emic* and *etic* are derived from the linguistic terms *phonemics* and *phonetics* respectively, descriptors of the dichotomy in all languages between the perceived alphabet in the mind of the native speakers and the actual sounds that they articulate when they speak. Pike and others subsequently broadened the application of *emic* and *etic* to all aspects of human behavior in culture, not simply language.

Emic	Etic
An *insider's* perspective	An *outsider's* perspective
In linguistics, they are the sounds I think I should say (a "t" in *top*, *pot*, and *butter*) based on phonemics or the correct alphabetical spelling	In linguistics, they are the sounds I actually say (an aspirated "t" in *top*; an unreleased "t" in *pot*, and a medial flapped "r" in *butter*) based on articulatory phonetics
Therefore, an emic unit is constant in the tacit mind of the insider despite its etic variability	Therefore, etic units are variable as per the outside observer despite their emic constancy

1. Pike, *Language in Relation to a Unified Theory of the Structure of Human Behavior.*

Emic	Etic
An *insider's* perspective	An *outsider's* perspective
Related to research methods, the primary data collection techniques are participant observation and in depth interviewing in the local vernacular	Related to research methods, the primary data collection technique is direct and indirect observation (often ethnographers will transition from emic to etic)
In linguistics, etic is used to discover emic	In culture, emic is used to discover etic
The research approach tends to be qualitative	The research approach tends to be quantitative
Categories of meaning are described based upon phenomenological definitions derived from the host society that are culturally and historically bound	Categories of meaning are described based upon scientific definitions from universal patterns of culture that are empirically documented across space/time history
Therefore, helpful descriptions are culture-specific, related to particular domains in the locale	Therefore, helpful descriptions are culture-general, related to broader comparisons across cultures
Constructs are grounded in self-understanding (consciously or unconsciously)	Constructs are predetermined from insights that apply equally well to all cultures
Consequently, emic systems are not necessarily transparent to the insider without exposure to others or training	Consequently, etic systems in a local cultural context are transparent to a trained outside observer
An example of emic variation is changing sports from football to baseball	An example of etic variation is playing an extra inning in a tied baseball game
Idealism (core worldview assumptions) is assumed to be the ultimate cause of observable behavior	Impersonal, non-ideational factors, especially material conditions are assumed to be the causes of observable behavior

Table E.1: Emic and Etic Perspectives

Appendix F

Value Dimensions of Culture

CULTURE MAY BE DEFINED AS a people's "learned, shared patterns of perception and behavior." A *dimension* of culture refers to an expressed feature of culture that is observable and measurable. Often dimensions of culture are presented in contrasting pairs, but the juxtaposition does not equate morality. In other words, it is not helpful to think of the dimensions of culture in terms of right or wrong.

The dimensions of culture have been analyzed and organized by qualitative research studies, including: Florence Kluckhohn and Fred Strodtbeck (1961), Geert Hofstede (1980, 1991, 2001), Fons Trompenaars (1997), Shalom Schwartz (1994), Robert House et al., at the University of Pennsylvania in the Global Leadership and Organizational Behavior Effectiveness [GLOBE] studies (2004), Michael Minkov (2013), and Edward T. Hall (1959, 1966, 1976).

Global Perspectives Consulting has consolidated the results of these studies into an integrated list of polarity pairs:

1. A focus on *task* versus people

2. *Monochronic* versus polychronic conception of time

3. *Egalitarian* versus hierarchical structure and function

4. *Low* versus high power distance

5. *Individualism* versus collectivism (group orientation)

6. *Speaker-oriented* speech versus associative involvement speech

7. The value of *change* versus tradition

8. *Low context* versus high context communication style

9. *Dichotomistic* versus holistic way of processing information

10. *Achieved* status versus ascribed

11. *Exposure of vulnerability* versus concealment of vulnerability ("face" saving)

12. *Guilt/innocence* pattern versus shame/honor

13. *Uncertainty avoidance* (rules) versus comfort with ambiguity

14. *Human intervention* versus fatalism as a propensity for control

15. *Abstract* conceptualist versus concrete relational/sequential learner

16. *Universalism* versus particularism

17. *Low physical contact* versus high

18. Display of emotion

19. Masculinity

20. *Materialism* versus religion

Do you notice any patterns? What links together? Does an individualist tend to be dichotomistic or holistic? Egalitarian or hierarchical? There are definite patterns displayed across cultures, verified through empirical research. Is there an order of priority? Young Yun Kim (2000) argues that the individualism/collectivism dimension is first. Geert Hofstede's (1980) research focused on five dimensions. Stella Ting-Toomey of California State University in Fullerton understands the critical importance of maintaining harmony through "face" negotiation.

A degree of complexity is needed to analyze cultures effectively. A cross-cultural worker must have some awareness of these dimensions, especially their form and function. The way a person behaves at work may not be the way she or he behaves at home or on the weekend. Urban and rural life may differ. Traveling only a short distance in India, one will encounter a new language and some changes in culture. As always, the first step in effective communication across cultures is to know oneself. Which of the dimensions best describe your values and behavior?

Appendix G

Max Weber

MAX WEBER (1864-1920) IS considered by many to be the *"Father of Modern Sociology".*[1] His emphasis on the historical influence of ideas encouraged sociologists to consider more than just a society's material culture and institutional structures. One of his primary interests was *Verstehen*, the emic understanding of the social actor in human exchange. Weber saw value in looking at the meaning social actors associate with behavior.

In 1904-5 Weber wrote a two-part article, later combined with an introduction (written in the year of his death) and footnotes in the seminal work, *The Protestant Ethic and the Spirit of Capitalism.*

If *capitalism* is a regular orientation to the achievement of profit through economic exchange[2], Weber saw a distinct modern iteration in the West, a rationalized capitalistic enterprise requiring a disciplined formally free labor force and regularized investment of capital.[3] Rather than a mere pursuit of gain through unlimited greed, Weber explores historical peculiarities[4] where Puritan entrepreneurs combine the impulse to accumulation with a positively frugal lifestyle, a rational capitalism that Weber

---

1. Montesquieu (1689-1755) is credited with the early assumption that disciplines like law, economics, or politics should be studied in relationship to each other rather than separately. This assumption was the seedling of sociology. Emile Durkheim (1858-1917) is also considered a principal architect of modern social science. He was impressed with the functional role of society's structure.

2. Weber, *The Protestant Ethic*, x.

3. Ibid., xi, xxxiv.

4. Ibid., 12.

understood was based upon a "this-worldly asceticism".[5] Such a notion stands in contrast to the Catholic ideal of an other-worldly monastic life with its objective of transcending the mundane.

The spirit (*Geist*) of capitalism is an attitude, an ethos, which seeks profit rationally and systematically in a self-controlled manner.[6]

The Protestant ethic Weber explores and describes is rooted in the Calvinistic doctrine of predestination. As such, Calvinism supplies the moral energy of the capitalist entrepreneur[7], a drive leading to duty in one's calling. The ideas become effective forces in history.[8]

Weber argues that in Calvinism, a sovereign God through fiat decree predestines ones to eternal salvation and others to damnation. The former are the elect of God. Both the faith to be saved and the resulting salvation are gifts of God given to the chosen. In reciprocal gratitude, the elect respond with a life of good works or rational labor[9], demonstrating one's effectual calling.[10] However, Weber also identifies other motivations. For example, one might be uncertain about election/salvation and consequently feel the need to prove one's redemption to the community of saints and larger world through good works. "The essential elements of the attitude which was there called the spirit of capitalism are the same as what we have just shown to be the content of the Puritan worldly asceticism".[11] Weber notes that authentic piety favors success in capitalism by insuring integrity and fostering habits of prudence.[12]

Interestingly, although Weber traces the historical interdependence of the Protestant ethic and the spirit of capitalism, especially from the sixteenth to the nineteenth century, by 1905 he concludes that capitalism rested on mechanical foundations, no longer in need of religious support. He describes the sense of personal duty as "the ghost of dead religious beliefs".[13] Going further he says, "The pursuit of wealth, stripped of its religious and ethical meaning, tends to become associated with purely mundane pas-

5. Ibid., xii, xxxi.
6. Ibid., 26–27.
7. Ibid., xiii.
8. Ibid., xviii.
9. Ibid., 107.
10. Ibid., 68–71.
11. Ibid., 123.
12. Ibid., 260.
13. Ibid., 124.

sions, which often actually give it the character of sport".[14] He seems also to claim that the spirit of capitalism now operates analogously to natural selection, lifting up and rewarding people who go to greater capitalistic extremes, casting out those who refuse to play the game. Weber characterizes victorious capitalism as an "iron cage"[15] and that "no one knows who will live in this cage in the future".[16][17]

14. Ibid., 124.

15. Ibid., 123.

16. Ibid., 124.

17. This appendix is co-authored by Christopher Strauss, a Professor of Literature at the University of New Mexico, Los Alamos, and Dr. Robert Strauss, Lead Faculty of Communication at Regis University in Denver, Colorado.

Appendix H

Edwards-Strauss-Steiner Model of Cultural Context Awareness of Self and Others

THE MODEL OF CULTURAL context awareness[1,2]:

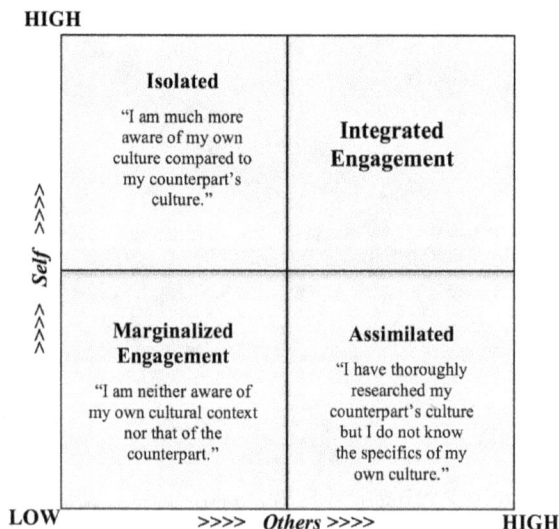

HIGH

Isolated	Integrated Engagement
"I am much more aware of my own culture compared to my counterpart's culture."	

Self >>>> ^^ >>>>

Marginalized Engagement	Assimilated
"I am neither aware of my own cultural context nor that of the counterpart."	"I have thoroughly researched my counterpart's culture but I do not know the specifics of my own culture."

LOW   >>>> *Others* >>>>   **HIGH**

Figure H.1: Model of Cultural Context Awareness

1. The terms *isolated* and *assimilated* in CCASO are borrowed from the research of John Berry. In his Model of Acculturation, the term "assimilation" means that an individual excludes his own culture and seeks to become part of the dominant society with its majority culture. "Isolated" means that an individual retains his own culture but does not seek to become part of the dominant society.

2. See http://ink.library.smu.edu.sg/lkcsb_research/4481 for academic research in "mindful engagement".

Bibliography

Achebe, Chinua. *Things Fall Apart*. New York: Anchor, 1959.

Agar, Michael. *Speaking of Ethnography*. Newbury Park, CA: Sage, 1992.

Aslan, Reza. *No god but God: The Origin, Evolution, and Future of Islam*. New York: Random House, 2011.

Authorship not Stated. *CBS: A Methodology for Presenting the Gospel to Oral Communicators*. Richmond, VA: International Mission Board of the Southern Baptist Convention, 2001.

Babbie, Earl. *The Practice of Social Research*. Belmont, CA: Wadsworth, 2013.

Barth, Karl. *Church Dogmatics: The Doctrine of the Word of God, Vol 1, Part 1*. Edinburgh, UK: T&T Clark, 1936.

Barton, George. "Temple of Herod." Jewishencyclopedia.com. http://www.jewish encyclopedia.com/articles/14304-temple-of-herod.

Bauckham, Richard. *Bible and Missions: Christian Witness in a Postmodern World*. Grand Rapids, MI: Baker Academic, 2003.

Beale, Gregory. *A New Testament Biblical Theology: An Unfolding of the Old Testament in the New*. Grand Rapids, MI: Baker Academic, 2011.

Beck, John. *God as Storyteller: Seeking Meaning in the Biblical Narrative*. Danvers, MA: Chalice, 2008.

Benedict, Ruth. *The Chrysanthemum and the Sword: Patterns of Japanese Culture*. Boston, MA: Houghton Mifflin, 1946/2005.

———. *The Patterns of Culture*. Boston, MA: Houghton Mifflin, 1934/2006.

Bennett, Milton. "Towards A Developmental Model of Intercultural Sensitivity." In *Education for the Intercultural Experience*, edited by R. Michael Paige, 21–71. Yarmouth, ME: Intercultural, 1993.

Berger, Peter. *The Sacred Canopy: Elements of a Sociological Theory of Religion*. New York: Anchor, 1967.

Bertalanffy, Ludwig. *General System Theory: Foundations, Development, and Applications*. New York: George Braziller, 1968.

Billings, J. Todd. *Union with Christ: Reframing Theology and Ministry for the Church*. Grand Rapids, MI: Baker Academic, 2011.

Block, Peter. *Stewardship: Choosing Service Over Self-Interest*. San Francisco, CA: Berrett-Koehler, 1993.

Bloom, Benjamin. *Taxonomy of Educational Objectives*. Boston, MA: Allyn and Bacon, 1956.

Book of Blessings. Washington, DC: International Committee on English in the Liturgy, 1988.

Boomershine, Thomas. *Story Journey: An Invitation to the Gospel as Storytelling*. Nashville, TN: Abingdon, 1988.

Booth, Wayne. *The Rhetoric of Fiction*. Chicago, IL: University of Chicago Press, 1983.

Bosch, David. *Transforming Mission: Paradigm Shifts in Theology of Mission*. Maryknoll, NY: Orbis, 1980.

Bradt, Kevin. *Story as a Way of Knowing*. Kansas City, MO: Sheed & Ward, 1997.

Brand, Sarah. "The Four P's of Exposition." Alpha.spellcaster.org. http://alpha.spellcaster. org/2010/08/02/the-four-ps-of-exposition.

Brueggemann, Walter. *The Creative Word: Canon as a Model for Biblical Education*. Philadelphia, PA: Fortress, 1982.

Bruner, Jerome. *Acts of Meaning*. Cambridge, MA: Harvard, 1990.

———. *The Culture of Education*. Cambridge, MA: Harvard University Press, 1996.

Bruner, Kurt. *The Divine Drama: Discovering Your Part in God's Story*. Wheaton, IL: Tyndale House, 2001.

Brunner, Emil. *Truth as Encounter*. Philadelphia, PA: Westminster, 1960.

Buber, Martin. *The Eclipse of God: Studies in the Relation Between Religion and Philosophy*. Amherst, NY: Humanity, 1952.

Callow, Kathleen. *Man and Message: A Guide to Meaning-Based Text Analysis*. New York: University Press of America, 1998.

Carson, Donald. *The Gagging of God: Christianity Confronts Pluralism*. Grand Rapids, MI: Zondervan, 1996.

Cass, Lewis. "Removal of the Indians." Nationalhumanitiescenter.org. http://national humanitiescenter.org/pds/triumphnationalism/expansion/text4/cassremoval.pdf (see lines 66–70).

Cassirer, Ernst. *The Philosophy of Symbolic Forms*. Yale: Yale University Press, 1955.

Chambert-Loir, Henri, and Anthony Reid. *The Potent Dead: Ancestors, Saints and Heroes in Contemporary Indonesia*. Honolulu, HI: University of Hawaii Press, 2002.

Clendenen, E. Ray. "Postholes, Postmodernism, and the Prophets: Toward a Textlinguistic Paradigm." *The Challenge of Postmodernism: An Evangelical Engagement*, edited by David Dockery, 132–47. Grand Rapids, MI: Baker Academic, 2001.

Confucius. *The Analects*. Translated by Raymond Dawson. New York: Oxford University Press, 2008.

Corbeill, Anthony. *Nature Embodied: Gesture in Ancient Rome*. Princeton: Princeton University Press, 2003.

Corbin, Juliet, and Anselm Strauss. *Basics of Qualitative Research*. Los Angeles, CA: Sage, 2007.

Creswell, John. *Qualitative Inquiry & Research Design: Choosing Among Five Approaches*. Thousand Oaks, CA: Sage, 2013.

Crossan, John. *The Dark Interval: Towards a Theology of Story*. Niles, IL: Argus, 1975.

Curtis, Brent, and John Eldridge. *The Sacred Romance: Drawing Closer to the Heart of God*. Nashville, TN: Thomas Nelson, 1997.

Davies, Douglas. *Anthropology and Theology*. New York: Berg, 1999.

Bibliography

Deacon, Terrence. *The Symbolic Species: The Co-Evolution of Language and the Brain*. New York: W. W. Norton, 1997.

Dewey, John. *Experience & Education*. New York: Touchstone, 1938.

———. *How We Think*. Boston, MA: Heath, 1933.

Dharma, Krishna. *Mahabharata: The Condensed Version of the World's Greatest Epic*. Badger, CA: Torchlight, 2000.

Dilthey, Wilhelm. *The Formation of the Historical World in the Human Sciences*. Princeton: Princeton University Press, 1895/2002.

Douglas, Mary. *Natural Symbols: Explorations in Cosmology*. New York: Pantheon, 1982.

———. *Purity and Danger: An Analysis of Concepts of Pollution and Taboo*. New York: Routledge, 1966/1996.

Drucker, Peter. "What Executives Should Remember." *Harvard Business Review* 84 (2006) 144–52.

Dunne, Peter. *Emotional Structure: Creating the Story Beneath the Plot*. Fresno, CA: Quill Driver, 2009.

Durkheim, Emile. *Selected Writings*. Cambridge: Cambridge University Press, late 1800s/1972.

Edersheim, Alfred. *The Temple: Its Ministry and Services as They Were at The Time of Christ*. Grand Rapids, MI: Eerdmans, 1986.

Egan, Kieran. *Teaching as Story Telling: An Alternative Approach to Teaching and Curriculum in the Elementary School*. Chicago, IL: University of Chicago Press, 1986.

Einstein, Albert. Herbert Spencer Lecture at Oxford University, 1933.

Eliade, Mercia. "Cosmogonic Myth and 'Sacred History.'" *Religious Studies* 2 (1967) 171–83.

Eliot, Thomas Stearns. *Four Quartets*. New York: Harcourt, Brace, 1943.

Fackre, Gabriel. "Christ's Ministry and Ours." In *The Laity in Ministry: The Whole People of God for the Whole World*, edited by George Peck and John Hoffman. Valley Forge, PA: Judson, 1984.

———. *Word in Deed: Theological Themes in Evangelism*. Grand Rapids, MI: William B. Eerdmans, 1975.

Fasokun, Thomas, et al. *The Psychology of Adult Learning in Africa*. Cape Town, Africa: Pearson Education, 2005.

Fetterman, David. *Ethnography: Step-by-Step*. Los Angeles, CA: Sage, 2010.

Fink, Dee. *Creating Significant Learning Experiences*. San Francisco, CA: Jossey-Bass, 2013.

Fisher, Walter. *Human Communication as Narration: Toward a Philosophy of Reason, Value, and Action*. Columbia: University of South Carolina Press, 1987.

Ford, Leighton. *The Power of Story: Rediscovering the Oldest, Most Natural Way to Reach People for Christ*. Colorado Springs, CO: NavPress, 1994.

Frankfort, Henri. *Ancient Egyptian Religion: An Introduction*. Columbia University Press, 2000.

Franklin, Benjamin. *Poor Richard's Almanack*. Philadelphia, PA: Publisher unknown, 1750.

Funk, Nathan, and Abdul Said. "Islam and the West: Narratives of Conflict and Conflict Transformation." *International Journal of Peace Studies* 9 (Spring/Summer 2004) 1–28.

Geertz, Clifford. *The Interpretation of Cultures*. New York: Basic, 1973.

———. *The Religion of Java*. Chicago, IL: University of Chicago Press, 1960.

Gezari, Vanessa. *The Tender Solider: A True Story of War and Sacrifice.* New York: Simon & Schuster, 2014.

Gnanakan, Ken. *Responsible Stewardship of God's Creation.* New York: World Evangelical Alliance, 2004.

Goetz, Judith (now Judith Preissle), and Margaret LeCompte. *Ethnography and Qualitative Design in Educational Research.* New York: Academic, 1984.

Goheen, Michael. "The Power of the Gospel and the Renewal of Scholarship." Biblicaltheology.ca. http://www.biblicaltheology.ca/blue_files/inaugural-goheen.pdf.

Goody, Jack. *The Interface between the Written and the Oral.* Cambridge: Cambridge University Press, 1987.

————. *The Theft of History.* Cambridge University Press, 2012.

Goss, Linda, and Clay Goss. *Jump and Say! A Collection of Black Storytelling.* New York: Touchstone, 1995.

Gotquestions.org. http://www.gotquestions.org/biblical-theology.html.

Greenleaf, Robert. *Servant Leadership: A Journey into the Nature of Legitimate Power and Greatness.* New York: Paulist, 1977.

Guthrie, Stan. *Missions in the Third Millennium: 21 Key Trends for the 21st Century.* Waynesboro, GA: Paternoster, 2000.

Hall, Edward. *Beyond Culture.* New York: Anchor, 1976.

————. *The Dance of Life: The Other Dimension of Time.* New York: Anchor, 1983.

————. *The Hidden Dimension.* New York: Anchor, 1966.

————. *The Silent Language.* New York: Anchor, 1959.

Halverson, Jeffery et al. *Master Narratives of Islamic Extremism.* New York, Palgrave Macmillan, 2011.

Harding, Barbara. "Towards a Poetics of Fiction: An Approach through Narrative." *Novel* 2 (1968) 5–14.

Harrison, Jim. A quote used in Chapter 5 that is commonly attributed to Harrison as does Simmons in *The Story Factor* (83).

Hauerwas, Stanley. *A Community of Character.* University of Notre Dame Press, 1981.

Hesselgrave, David. "Christian Contextualization and Biblical Theology." Paper delivered at the Evangelical Missiological Society, Midwest meeting, March 14–15, 1997.

————. *Communicating Christ Cross-Culturally: An Introduction to Missionary Communication, Second Edition.* Grand Rapids, MI: Zondervan, 1991.

Hiebert, Paul. *Transforming Worldviews: An Anthropological Understanding of How People Change.* Grand Rapids, MI: Baker Academic, 2008.

Hiebert, Paul, et al. *Understanding Folk Religion: A Christian Response to Popular Beliefs and Practices.* Grand Rapids, MI: Baker, 1999.

Hofstede, Geert. *Cultures and Organizations: Software of the Mind.* New York: McGraw-Hill, 1997.

————. *Culture's Consequences: International Differences in Work-Related Values.* Beverly Hills CA: Sage, 1980.

Homer. *Iliad.* Translated by Stanley Lombardo. Indianapolis, IN: Hackett, 1997.

————. *Odyssey.* Translated by Stanley Lombardo. Indianapolis, IN: Hackett, 2000.

House, Robert, et al. *Culture, Leadership, and Organizations: The GLOBE Study of 62 Societies.* Thousand Oaks, CA: Sage, 2004.

Howard, George. "A Narrative Approach to Thinking, Cross-Cultural Psychology, and Psychotherapy." *American Psychologist* 46 (1991) 187–97.

BIBLIOGRAPHY

Jacobson, Jennifer. *Reading Response for Fiction*. New York: Scholastic, 2008.

Johnson, Mark. *The Body in the Mind: The Bodily Basis of Meaning, Imagination, and Reason*. Chicago, IL: University of Chicago Press, 1990.

Jones, Tony. *Postmodern Youth Ministry*. Grand Rapids, MI: Zondervan, 2001.

Kearney, Michael. *World View*. Novato, CA: Chandler & Sharp, 1984.

Kennedy, X. J., et al. *Handbook of Literature Terms: Literature, Language, Theory*. New York: Pearson, 2005.

Kernen, Robert. *Building Better Plots*. Cincinnati, OH: Writer's Digest, 1999.

Kettner, Peter, et al. *Designing and Managing Programs: An Effectiveness-Based Approach*. Los Angeles, CA: Sage, 2012.

Kidd, Warren. *Culture and Identity*. New York: Palgrave Macmillan, 2002.

Kidwell, Clara, et al. *A Native American Theology*. Maryknoll, NY: Orbis, 2001.

Kirkpatrick, Don. *Evaluating Training Programs: The Four Levels*. San Francisco, CA: Berrett-Koehler, 2006.

————. *No-Nonsense Communication*. Brookfield, WI: K & M, 1978.

Klink III, Edward, and Darion Lockett. *Understanding Biblical Theology: A Comparison of Theory and Practice*. Grand Rapids, MI: Zondervan, 2012.

Kluckhohn, Florence, and Fred Strodtbeck. *Variations in Value Orientations*. Evanston, IL: Row, Peterson, 1961.

Kolb, David. *Experiential Learning: Experience as the Source of Learning and Development*. Upper Saddle River, NJ: Prentice Hall, 1984.

Kostenburger, Andreas. *The Missions of Jesus and the Disciples According to the Fourth Gospel*. Grand Rapids, MI: William B. Eerdmans, 1998.

Kraft, Charles. *Christianity in Culture: A Study in the Dynamic Biblical Theologizing in Cross-Cultural Perspective*. Maryknoll, NY: Orbis, 1979.

Kunnie, Julian, and Nomalungelo Goduka, eds. *Indigenous People's Wisdom and Power: Affirming Our Knowledge through Narratives*. Burlington, VT: Ashgate, 2006.

Lamb, Nancy. *The Art and Craft of Storytelling: A Comprehensive Guide to Classic Writing Techniques*. Cincinnati, OH: Writer's Digest, 2008.

Lasn, Kalle. *Culture Jam*. New York: HarperCollins, 2000.

Lassiter, James. "African Culture and Personality." *African Studies Quarterly* 3 (1999) 29–35.

LeCompte, Margaret, and Jean Schensul. *Analyzing & Interpreting Ethnographic Data*. Walnut Creek, CA: Altamira, 1999.

Levi-Strauss, Claude. *The Savage Mind*. Chicago, IL: University Chicago Press, 1966.

Lewis, C. S. *The Literary Impact of the Authorized Version*. Philadelphia, PA: Fortress, 1963.

Lincoln, Bruce. *Holy Terrors: Thinking About Religion After September 11*. Chicago, IL: University of Chicago Press, 2003.

Lingenfelter, Sherwood. *Transforming Culture: A Challenge for Christian Mission*. Grand Rapids, MI: Baker Academic, 1998.

Lipman, Doug. *Improving Your Storytelling: Beyond the Basics for All Who Tell Stories in Work or Play*. Atlanta, GA: August House, 1999.

MacDonald, Margaret. *The Story-Teller's Start-Up Book*. Little Rock, AR: August, 1993.

MacIntyre, Alasdair. *After Virtue: A Study in Moral Theory*. University of Notre Dame Press, 2007.

Madden, Raymond. *Being Ethnographic: A Guide to the Theory and Practice of Ethnography*. Los Angeles, CA: Sage, 2011.

Mair, Miller. "Psychology as Storytelling." *International Journal of Personal Construct Psychology* 1 (1988) 125–38.

Martin, Judith, and Tom Nakayama. *Intercultural Communication in Contexts*. New York: McGraw-Hill, 2013.

Maslow, Abraham. A Theory of Human Motivation. *Psychological Review* 50 (1943) 370–96.

McCroskey, James. *An Introduction to Rhetorical Communication*. 9th ed. Englewood Cliffs, NJ: Prentice-Hall, 2005.

McCurdy, David, et al. *The Cultural Experience: Ethnography in Complex Society*. New York: Waveland, 2004.

McKee, Robert. *Story: Style, Structure, Substance, and the Principles of Screenwriting*. New York: Harper-Collins, 1997.

Merriam, Sharan, and Gabo Nsteane. "Transformational Learning in Botswana: How Culture Shapes the Process." *Adult Education Quarterly* (2008) 183–97.

Meyers, Marvin. *Christianity Confronts Culture: A Strategy for Cross-Cultural Evangelism*. Grand Rapids, MI: Zondervan, 1987.

Miller, Donald. *Story and Context: An Introduction to Christian Education*. Nashville, TN: Abingdon, 1987.

Miller, Dorothy. *Simply the Story Handbook*, 6e. Hemet, CA: The God's Story Project, 2016.

Minkov, Michael. *Cross-Cultural Analysis: The Science and Art of Comparing the World's Modern Societies and Their Cultures*. Los Angeles, CA: Sage, 2013.

Morson, Gary. "Forward: Intelligence and the Storytelling Process." In *Tell Me a Story: Narrative and Intelligence*, edited by Roger Schank. Northwestern University Press, 2000.

Muller, Roland. *Honor & Shame: Unlocking the Door*. Bloomington, IN: Xlibris, 2001.

Mumford, Lewis. *Technics and Civilization*. New York: Harcourt, Brace, 1934.

Needham, Rodney. *Belief, Language, and Experience*. Oxford: Basil Blackwell, 1972.

Neff, David. "Remember the Red Sea: Why Not Capitalize on the Richness and Mystery of Our Ancient Symbols?" *Christianity Today* 55 (2011) 68–69.

Nehru, Jawaharlal. *The Discovery of India*. Calcutta, India: The Signet, 1946.

Newbigin, Leslie. *The Gospel in a Pluralistic Society*. Grand Rapids, MI: William B. Eerdmans, 1989.

Nida, Eugene. *Customs and Cultures: Anthropology for Christian Missions*. Pasadena, CA: William Carey Library, 1954/1975.

Niebuhr, Reinhold. *A Nation So Conceived*. Westport, CT: Greenwood, 1963.

Ong, Walter. *Orality and Literacy*. London: Routledge, 2002.

Osborne, Grant. *The Hermeneutical Spiral: A Comprehensive Introduction to Biblical Interpretation*. Downers Grove, IL: Intervarsity, 2006.

Palmer, Parker. *The Courage to Teach: Exploring the Inner Landscape of a Teacher's Life*. San Francisco, CA: Jossey-Bass, 1998.

Parkman, Francis. *The Oregon Trail*. Oxford University Press, 2008.

Parks, David. "Introduction to Flashback." Flashbacktojesus.blogspot.com. http://flashbacktojesus.blogspot.com/2010/06/introduction-to-flashback.html.

Pellowski, Anne. *The World of Storytelling: A Practical Guide to the Origins, Development, and Applications of Storytelling*. Bronx, NY: H. W. Wilson, 1991.

Pelto, Pertti, and Gretel Pelto. *Anthropological Research: The Structure of Inquiry*. Cambridge University Press, 1978.

Perry, Simon. "How Biblical is Expository Preaching?" Simonperry.org. http://Simonperry. Org.Uk/Exposition/4550415875.

Pike, Kenneth. *Language in relation to a unified theory of the structure of human behavior.* Berlin, Germany: De Gruyter Mouton, 1967/2015.

———. *Phonemics: A Technique for Reducing Languages to Writing.* Ann Arbor, MI: University of Michigan Press, 1976.

Plato. *Phaedo.* Translated by David Gallop. Oxford: Oxford University Press, c. 360BCE/2009.

Popovich, Francis. "The Old Testament and a Theology of God." *Notes on Scripture in Use and Language Programs* 23 (1990) 32–36.

Postman, Neil. *Amusing Ourselves to Death: Public Discourse in the Age of Show Business.* New York: Penguin, 1985.

Qutb, Sayyid. *Milestones.* New Delhi, India: Islamic Book Service, 2009.

Ramachandran, Jayakumar. "Current Political and Missions Landscape in India: A Missiological Appraisal for Future Missions." *Evangelical Missions Quarterly* 52 (2016) 282–90.

Redfield, Robert. *The Primitive World and Its Transformations.* Ithaca, NY: Cornell University Press, 1953.

Ricoeur, Paul. *Interpretation Theory: Discourse and the Surplus of Meaning.* Fort Worth, TX: Texas Christian University Press, 1976.

———. *Time and Narrative, Volume 1.* Chicago, IL: University of Chicago Press, 1985.

Robinson, Haden. *Biblical Preaching: The Development and Delivery of Expository Messages.* Grand Rapids, MI: Baker, 1980.

Ryken, Leland. *How to Read the Bible as Literature . . . And Get More Out of It.* Grand Rapids, MI: Zondervan, 1984.

———. *Words of Delight: A Literary Introduction to the Bible.* Grand Rapids, MI: Baker, 2005.

Sahih Muslim Book 26, Hadith 5427. Hadithcollection.com. http.//www.hadithcollection. com.

Sanskrit Religions Institute. Sanskrit.org. http://www.sanskrit.org.

Sawyer, Ruth. *The Way of the Storyteller.* New York: Penguin, 1942.

SBC Life: Journal of the Southern Baptist Convention, May 2013.

Schank, Roger. *Tell Me a Story.* Evanston, IL: Northwestern University Press, 2000.

Schattner, Frank. *The Wheel Model: Catalyzing Sustainable Church Multiplication Movements.* Rocklin, CA: Jessup, 2014.

Schwartz, Shalom. "Are There Universal Aspects in the Content and Structure of Values?" *Journal of Social Issues* 50 (1994) 19–45.

Seymour, D. Bruce. *Creating Stories That Connect: A Pastor's Guide to Storytelling.* Grand Rapids, MI: Kregel, 2007.

Shannon, Claude, and Warren Weaver. *The Mathematical Theory of Communication.* Urbana, IL: The University of Illinois Press, 1949.

Shaw, Susan. *Storytelling in Religious Education.* Birmingham, AL: Religious Education, 1999.

Simmel, Georg. *The Sociological Significance of the "Stranger".* Chicago, IL: University of Chicago Press, 1921.

Simmons, Annette. *The Story Factor: Inspiration, Influence, and Persuasion Through the Art of Storytelling* 2e. Cambridge, MA: Basic, 2006.

———. *Whoever Tells the Best Story WINS: How to Use Your Own Stories to Communicate with Power and Impact.* New York: AMACOM, 2007.

Slack, Jim, and J. O. Terry. *Chronological Bible Storying.* Richmond, VA: International Mission Board of the Southern Baptist Convention, 1997.

Spradley, James. *The Ethnographic Interview.* New York: Harcourt Brace Jovanovich College, 1979.

Steffen, Tom. *The Facilitator Era: Beyond Pioneer Church Multiplication.* Eugene, OR: Wipf & Stock, 2011.

———. "Flawed Evangelism and Church Planting." *Evangelical Missions Quarterly* 34 (1998) 428–35.

———. "Foundational Roles of Symbol and Narrative in the (Re)Construction of Reality and Relationship." *Missiology: An International Review* 26 (1998) 477–94.

———. *Passing the Baton: Church Planting that Empowers.* La Habra, CA: Center for Organizational & Ministry Development, 1997.

Steffen, Tom, and J. O. Terry. "The Sweeping Story of Scripture Taught through Time." *Missiology: An International Review* 35 (2007) 315–35.

Stolovitch, Harold, and Erica Keeps. *Telling Ain't Training.* Alexandria, VA: ASTD, 2001.

Strauss, Christopher. "Vyasa's Oceanic Mind: An Approach to Reading the Mahabharata." Paper submitted in the Mahabharata Preceptorial at St. John's College, Santa Fe, New Mexico, 2009.

Strauss, Robert. "Case Study of New Tribes Integral Training Program." In *Integral Ministry Training—Design and Evaluation,* edited by Robert Brynjolfson and Jonathan Lewis, 178–83. Pasadena, CA: WEA-William Carey Library, 2006.

———. "Culture." Gpccolorado.com. http://www.gpccolorado.com/culture.

———. "The Emerging Geography of Global Christianity: New Places, Faces and Perceptions." In *The Changing Religion Map: Sacred Places, Identities, Practices, and Politics,* edited by Stanley Brunn, 1781–94. Dordrecht, Netherlands: Springer, 2014.

———. "Experiential Learning." Gpccolorado.com. http://www.gpccolorado.com/experiential-learning/.

———. "Fundamentos Para Guiar el Diseño de la Capacitación." Traducido por Yamina Gava y Barbara Compañy. In *Manual de Capacitación Transcultural: Una Guía Orientadora Los Procesos de Capacitación Misionera Integral,* edited by Omar Gava and Robert Strauss, 41–63. Villa Carlos Paz, Argentina: Recursos Estratégicos Globales, 2009.

———. "Tribal Church Planter Profile." *International Journal of Frontier Missions* 15 (April–June 1998) 87–89.

———. "Worldview." Gpccolorado.com. http://www.gpccolorado.com/worldview.

Strauss, Robert, and Tom Steffen. "Change the Worldview . . . Change the World." *Evangelical Missions Quarterly* 45 (2009) 458–464.

Sweet, Leonard. *Post-Modern Pilgrims: First Century Passion for the 21st Century Church.* Nashville, TN: Broadman & Holman, 2000.

Terry, J. O. *In Defense of Storying.* http://www.chronologicalbiblestorying.com.

———. *A Literate Walk Down an Oral Road.* http://www.chronologicalbiblestorying.com.

Thrall, Bill, et al. *The Ascent of a Leader: How Ordinary Relationships Develop Extraordinary Character and Influence.* San Francisco, CA: Jossey-Bass, 1999.

Ting-Toomey, Stella. *Communicating Across Cultures.* New York: The Guilford, 1999.

Tisdell, Elizabeth. *Exploring Spirituality and Culture in Adult and Higher Education*. State College, PA: Pennsylvania State University, 2003.

Transforming Business Operations. Tbointl.com. http://www.tbointl.com/training.

Trompenaars, Fons, and Charles Hampden-Turner. *Riding the Waves of Culture: Understanding Cultural Diversity in Global Business*. New York, McGraw-Hill, 1997.

Turner, Victor. *Dramas, Fields, and Metaphors: Symbolic Action in Human Society*. Ithaca, NY: Cornell University Press, 1974.

Vanhoozer, Kevin. *The Drama of Doctrine: A Canonical Linguistic Approach to Christian Theology*. Louisville, KY: Westminster John Knox, 2005.

————. *Is There Meaning in This Text? The Bible, the Reader, and the Morality of Literary Knowledge*. Grand Rapids, MI: Zondervan, 1998.

Walker, William. *Progressive Revelation*. Hollywood, FL: Span, 1971.

Wallace, Anthony. *Culture and Personality*. New York: Random House, 1970.

Wangerin, Walter. *The Book of God: The Bible as a Novel*. Grand Rapids, MI: Zondervan, 1996.

Ward, Glenn. *Teach Yourself Postmodernism*. Chicago, IL: McGraw-Hill, 2003.

Ward, Ted. Presentation about andragogy at the IFMA/EFMA Annual Conference. Orlando, FL, 1992.

Warneck, Gustav. *Outline of a History of Protestant Missions from the Reformation to the Present Time: A Contribution to Modern Church History*. New York: Fleming H. Revell, 1901.

Weber, Max. *The Protestant Ethic and the Spirit of Capitalism*. London: Routledge, 1895/2001.

Wendig, Chuck. "25 Ways to Make Exposition Your Bitch." http://terribleminds.com/ramble/2011/08/09/25-ways-to-make-exposition-your-bitch/.

White, Leslie. *The Science of Culture: A Study of Man and Civilization*. New York: Grove, 1949.

Wiesel, Elie. *The Gates of the Forest*. New York: Schocken, 1966.

Wiggins, Grant, and Jay McTighe. *Understanding by Design*. Alexandria, VA: Association for Supervision and Curriculum Development, 1998.

Willis, Avery. *Making Disciples of Oral Learners*. Lima, NY: Elim, 2007.

Wolcott, Harry. *Ethnography: A Way of Seeing*. New York: Rowman & Littlefield, 2008.

Wolfer, Loreen. *Real Research: Conducting and Evaluating Research in the Social Sciences*. Boston, MA: Pearson, 2006.

Wright, Christopher. *The Mission of God: Unlocking the Bible's Grand Narrative*. Downers Grove, IL: InterVarsity, 2006.

Wright, N. T. *The New Testament and the People of God*. Minneapolis, MN: Fortress, 1992.

Yun Kim, Young. *Becoming Intercultural: An Integrative Theory of Communication and Cross-Cultural Adaptation*. Thousand Oaks, CA: Sage, 2000.

Index

Abstract conceptualization, 13, 74, 97, 109n10

Acculturation, 172

Achebe, Chinua, 16n11, 17n13

Agar, Michael, 91n22

Animism, animistic, 13, 16, 17, 21, 22, 23, 68n67, 114, 148

Apostle Paul, Paul, 9–10, 12n15, 30, 36, 38n16, 88–89, 103n3, 121, 124, 131, 134, 136

Argentina, 12, 70, 94, 102, 142, 161

Arizona State University, xi, 44n6, 47, 77, 95, 149

Aslan, Reza, 3, 5

Assimilation, 172n1

Assumption(s), xvi–xviii, 7, 14, 15, 17, 19, 22–23, 28–39, 43–49, 51, 53, 55, 66, 70, 72, 75n89, 76n90, 84, 86, 92, 95–96, 100, 107, 109n10, 112, 119, 127–28, 131–33, 136, 138, 140, 143, 147, 149, 153, 162–63, 166, 169n1

"Auto pilot", 28, 163

Babbie, Earl, 99n32

Barth, Karl, 132n9

Barton, George, xiiin2

Bauckham, Richard, 68

Beale, Gregory, 132n10

Beck, John, 139

Behavior(s), xvi, 14, 16, 21, 24, 26, 28, 38, 45–46, 48, 50–52, 54–55, 58, 61, 91–92, 95, 97–99, 118–19, 125, 142, 145, 152–53, 155, 157, 159–69

Outward observable behavior, xvi, 46, 48, 157

Benedict, Ruth, 155–56

Bennett, Milton, 82n2

Berger, Peter, 60n8

Bertalanffy, Ludwig van, 48n18

Bible, xvii, 4, 9, 11–12, 17, 20, 23, 28, 30, 32–39, 65–66, 68–72, 76n90, 78, 82–84, 90, 99–100, 106, 118, 120, 124, 129–35, 138–39, 142, 144, 146, 148

Billings, J. Todd, 54n35

Bisorio people, 76n90

Block, Peter, 65

Bloom, Benjamin, 116–17

Bloom's Taxonomy of Cognitive Learning, 116–17

Boomershine, Thomas, 61n16, 75n89, 133

Booth, Wayne, 74n84

Bosch, David, 87

Bradt, Kevin, xvin6, 53n34, 60, 64–65, 67

Brand, Sarah, 34n7

Brevity, 12, 28, 36n10, 126, 138

Brueggemann, Walter, 60

Bruner, Jerome, 63–64

Index

Ford, Leighton, 105
Form, function, and meaning, 108
Frame of reference, 56, 86–87
Frankfort, Henri, 68
Franklin, Benjamin, 25, 83
Funk, Nathan, and Abdul Said, 5

Geertz, Clifford, 18n14, 51
Gezari, Vanessa, 6n3
Global Perspectives Consulting, xi, 153, 156, 160, 167
Gnanakan, Ken, 67
Goetz, Judith (now Judith Preissle), and Margaret LeCompte, 91n22
Goheen, Michael, 66
Good Seed International, 14
Goody, Jack, 83n4, 144
Gospel, xiv–xv, 5–6, 12n5, 16, 17, 33, 36, 61n15, 69, 76n90, 87, 105, 126, 134, 137
Goss, Linda, and Clay Goss, 61n14
Greenleaf, Robert, 84n9
Grounded theory, 91n19, 152
Guatemala, 12, 21, 90
Guilt/righteousness pattern of culture, 27, 109n10, 156–57, 168
Guthrie, Stan, 140n24

Hadith, 19, 20, 88
Hall, Edward T., 83, 143, 167
Halverson, Jeffery, 44n6, 91
Harding, Barbara, 52
Harmony, 75, 156–58, 168
Harrison, Jim, 65
Hauerwas, Stanley, 63n27
Hesselgrave, David, xv, 53
Hiebert, Paul, 43, 47, 49–50, 52, 69, 119
Hierarchical, 27, 68n67, 109, 157, 162, 167–68
    Maslow's hierarchy, 115
Hinduism, 13, 114
Hofstede, Geert, 143, 167–68
Holistic, xix, 25, 38, 58, 66, 68n67, 70, 108, 146, 149, 157, 168
Holy Spirit, xviii, 32, 35–39, 54n35, 72, 100, 129, 133–36, 144, 146, 148
Homer, 33

Honor/shame pattern of culture, 26–27, 55, 81, 115n2, 155–58, 162n3, 168
Host society, xviii, 6, 11n4, 28, 34, 38, 53–55, 75n89, 81, 82n3, 84–85, 87, 92n26, 96, 99, 102, 104, 108, 131, 134–35, 137, 141–42, 151, 163, 166
House, Robert, 167
Howard, George, 51

Identity, 26, 35, 47, 63, 115, 121, 138, 152, 156–57, 161–62
India, 12–16, 36n10, 112–14, 142, 147, 154, 163, 168
India Institute of Missiology, 13, 15
Individualism, 25, 46, 109n10, 157, 167
Indonesia, 12, 18, 59, 61, 70
Innocence, 109n10, 168
Insider, 8, 83n8, 165–66
Institution(s), xvi, 29, 45n9, 46, 48, 55, 95–96, 108, 119, 125–26, 138, 152, 157, 162, 169
Intercultural communication, xviii, 6, 35, 54, 70, 76, 83, 149
International Academy of Intercultural Research (IAIR), 77
Interpretation, 37, 71, 74, 131–32
Interview, 12, 81, 115n2, 152–53, 166
Islam, 5, 15, 24, 44n6, 54, 68, 88, 91, 93, 102, 148n2
Isnad and matn, 88–90

Jacobson, Jennifer, 37
Jesus, Jesus Christ, Son of God, xiii, xv, xix, 6, 14, 16, 20, 33, 36, 51, 54n35, 72n78, 75n89, 88, 110, 121, 125, 130–31, 134–37, 140, 147, 150
Johnson, Mark, 66
Jones, Tony, 37
Justice, 94, 155–57

Kearney, Michael, 45, 47, 143
Kennedy, X. J., 50
Kernen, Robert, 37
Kettner, Peter, 36

Index

INDEX

www.ingramcontent.com/pod-product-compliance
Lightning Source LLC
Chambersburg PA
CBHW061733270326
41928CB00011B/2219